PARISH RITUALS FOR KEY MOMENTS

Eileen Deegan CSB

Parish Rituals
for Key Moments

the columba press

First published in 2005 by
the columba press
55A Spruce Avenue, Stillorgan Industrial Park, Blackrock, Co Dublin

Cover by Bill Bolger
Origination by The Columba Press
Printed in Ireland by Colour Books Ltd, Dublin

ISBN 1 85607 486 2

Contents

Preface

The rituals in this book were created and celebrated in Rivermount Parish, Finglas South, Dublin over a period of nine years. In this community, many people are committed to God in the widest sense but do not seem to relate to the usual church services. These rituals then are an attempt to reach such people and touch into the key moments in their lives across the parish in any given year. I have found that many people come and are drawn into a sense of the sacred. They participate wholeheartedly and willingly in these celebrations.

Over the years I have shared some of the ideas included with other interested parishes and at workshops in All Hallows College (Dublin) and elsewhere. In fact, this book came about as a result of people's enthusiastic response to their involvement in such rituals. Many have suggested that these be made available as a resource for those who are searching for ways forward to connect real life issues with church ritual.

It is presented not as an expert work but rather as the fruit of our efforts to touch into the issues affecting people's lives at key moments. I can say with conviction that these have worked well for us in our parish.

I have also included some other services: Reconciliation Services which have been used in the parish during Advent and Lent; A Funeral Ritual which can be adapted and made personal for each bereaved family; A revised rite for the celebration of the Sacrament of Confirmation, and finally a House Blessing.

Most of the rituals in this book can be created, celebrated and led by lay leaders in parishes. These are an example of what has been done in one place. It is my wish that people using this book will be inspired to draw on their own experience to create meaningful rituals.

Introduction

The various stages in the individual and family lifecycle are indeed significant and sacred moments. These need to be highlighted and celebrated in our parishes. I suggest that we explore and exploit the wonder, marvel and awesomeness of some of the key moments in life, by developing sacred rituals that express what is happening at the inner core of the individual or community.

It may be a ritual with which we're already familiar – a Mass in November for those who died in that year or the celebration of weddings, baptisms, communions, confirmations and funerals. A new format has to move us beyond the set rituals. Many people today are not 'in touch' with church. Others who still come to services are not 'touched' or nourished by them. Therefore we need to explore other ways within church of connecting with the needs of people at the significant moments in their lives.

So much of liturgy, as people experience it, is centred on the Eucharist. Sometimes it is too much 'of the head' – it doesn't reach people at the level of everyday experience. Liturgy and life do need to connect.

We often refer to life as a journey and talk of the different stages in the lifecycle; we look at the journey of life with its hopes and fears, its ups and downs. That's the material of life for each of us and for all in the parish community.

We need to ask: How can we create liturgy/ rituals that touch the inner spirit of people at the key moments in their lives?

George Carey, the Archbishop of Canterbury, reflecting on the outpouring of feeling at the time of Princess Diana's death, commented: 'We want rituals that give people space instead of confining them within a set form on a take-it or leave-it basis. There is demand for services which creatively address special concerns or points of life, from baptisms or marriages to care of the environment.'

In the context of parish life we need to see when and how to create rituals that are important to people at these significant times in their lives. We recall how in the past people had devotions, benediction, processions and novenas which touched them or involved them in significant ways. There is a real void now for many people. So, what we are trying to do is to help people find God and discover the spiritual in the 'bits and pieces of everyday.' (Patrick Kavanagh).

Meaningful rituals put us in touch with the sacred and holy in ourselves and in life around us. The symbols, words, music and reflections used, create an atmosphere where people experience the sacred in those special moments.

So the first question is: What events are important to ritualise in a parish? The answer to that determines the themes of the rituals and then all the other elements develop and enhance them.

Then there is a need to think of various ways to develop the theme in order to meet the needs of the participants.

It is helpful to generate ideas for the theme with a group of interested parishioners and parish leaders. The question is: What are we hoping to evoke from the participants in the ritual?

Good ritual will inevitably create and develop community in the group gathered.

The key elements in any ritual will include:
A Symbol
Meditation
Scripture
Music
Movement
Prayer Together

The Symbol
Symbols carry the meaning. They are the tools for developing the theme. It is important to use symbols that are integral to people's lives.

We can revitalise the familiar symbols, e.g. water, oil, candles, rosary etc., by using them in a new way. All creation is holy; symbols then can be any aspect of creation, e.g. stones, leaves, seashells, flower bulbs etc.

9

Whatever symbol is chosen for a particular ritual is invested with meaning during the ritual and particularly at the time of the guided reflection / meditation.

Guided Meditation/Gentle Reflection

Meditation is central to any ritual. This helps people to tap into their inner selves, to travel within to their still point, to reflect on their experience and to find that God is with them at the very depth of their particular life story. Verses or words of scripture are integrated into the guided reflection and hopefully participants will hear that Word spoken into their experience. Throughout the meditation, they are holding or looking at the symbol and in the context of the meditation this is becoming something especially meaningful for them at this time in their lives. Soft, background music enhances the meditation. It puts people at their ease and helps them to centre themselves.

Scripture

Pieces of scripture need to be chosen carefully, ensuring that they relate to the theme being developed. A few verses, read slowly and reflectively, can often mean more than a very lengthy reading. Sometimes the scripture can be read using a few voices or in the form of a dialogue. It's important that participants are helped to integrate the Word of God into their lived experience.

Music

Songs and music chosen need to be in keeping with the theme and the occasion being ritualised. Sometimes, I believe, it's good to have a song played. It's also good if people can sing one or two songs during the ritual as the participation of all in singing is very important.

Movement

Some form of movement is important as a way of involving people actively in ritual. Sometimes, it can be a procession after the guided meditation, to place the symbol in the sacred space, to light a candle or to bless with water. In some rituals a circle dance can be done by a group or a liturgical dance can be incorporated. Again this can involve the entire group or a small group. In doing so, it is important to ensure that people feel comfortable doing what is required. It needs to be introduced as another form of prayer.

Prayer Together
This involves the entire group of participants drawing together the strands of the ritual in a communal prayer. It's good to have a prayer printed for each one. This needs to be prepared in advance by the planning group. At other stages in the ritual, space needs to be created for spontaneous prayer by participants.

Sometimes at the end of the meditation it may be opportune to ask people to share a prayer, a thought or a reflection that moved within them during the guided reflection.

The above six elements are key to most rituals.

There are additional elements which can be included. The sharing of a story can be very powerful in the context of some rituals, as in the celebration for Valentine's Day when a couple may share some of their story of love and loving. At the service for those who have had a miscarriage or still birth, a parent or parents could share their pain of loss and how they cope. It is a way of helping other participants in the ritual to reflect more deeply on their own story.

Setting the tone of the ritual
The ritual space must create an environment of welcome and comfort. I believe people coming into the room must be struck by the general atmosphere before any words are spoken. I suggest that the main church building is not always the most suitable space for such rituals. It tends to be too large given that smaller, more specific groups attend particular rituals. If there is a room off the church or in the parish house that is more suitable then I suggest that venue be used.

Cloths, pictures, lighting, soft music, symbols need to be in place before people arrive. The welcoming atmosphere, the general décor, the arrangement of the chairs are vitally important if an appropriate ambience is to be effectively created.

This all involves good planning and hard work!

Brigid Brings the Spring

General Comment

In the Celtic world, the spring equinox is very important. In our Christian tradition the feast of St Brigid on 1 February ushers in the springtime in the northern hemisphere.

It is a time of hope, of new life, of rebirth. It is a good time to acknowledge God as the source of all life and to celebrate as a faith community the ways in which Brigid of Kildare challenges us in our time to be channels of hope, life, justice, peace, faith and healing in the lives of others around us.

The preparation for this celebration needs careful planning. The involvement of local people and local schools in the making of St Brigid's crosses adds greatly to the overall participation. The decoration and general preparation of the room in which it will take place is vital. The use of spring flowers, lights, pictures and colour helps to create the ambience for a meaningful celebration.

It is our experience that this gathering is very much appreciated by many people. The spirituality of St Brigid touches into the psyche of people and so they relate very well to this celebration. It is also an ideal time to involve young people as the various elements of the ritual appeal to them.

The following ritual is rather long and it contains a veriety of reflections. I suggest that one could pick and choose from these rich resources in the creation of a ritual to suit one's purpose in a parish or any other group situation.

The songs are merely suggestions. There are many songs which one can choose from other sources that also focus on the themes presented.

It is a good idea to have a sheet with words of songs and some prayer or reflections for all participants so as to ensure greater involvement in the ritual.

Structure of the Ritual
- Presentation of four elements of Creation
- Presentation of some qualities of Brigid
- Presentation and blessing of St Brigid's crosses
- Blessing with water from St Brigid's well
- A choice of reflective poems on Brigid
- A final blessing

Building up of the Sacred Space: (lights down low and background music)
This is Brigid's Festival. Brigid brings the Spring.

We welcome the Brigid Light into our midst as we gather to share the light of hope and inspiration that will grow with the growing year.

We honour St Brigid of Kildare, Patroness of our country, whose feast-day on 1 February ushers in the springtime in our northern hemisphere.

This fifth-century woman has continued to inspire and encourage people in Ireland and elsewhere for over 1500 years.

PRESENTATION OF FOUR ELEMENTS OF CREATION

Going back to Brigid's time and before, our ancestors had a deep respect for the elements of creation: earth, air, water, fire.

Instrumental music is played

N: We invite you now to relax and allow the ancient elements of creation – the earth, air, water and fire to encircle us, to ring round us, gracing us with their wisdom, connecting us to each other and to the whole community of life, that is our universe.

Pause (music continues)

N: We celebrate the gift of the earth.
N carries in a sod of clay
Every part of this earth is sacred. From ancient times the earth has been portrayed as feminine. Humankind experiences the earth as life-giving, nourishing, rhythmic and fertile.

We are invited to walk gently on this earth and read her wisdom in every leaf and rock and field and care for her with tender respect.

On her lands we walk and work, play and love. In the words of singer and songwriter, Dolores Keane:

It's the land that is our wisdom,
it's the land that shines us through,
it's the land that feeds our children.
You cannot own the land,
The land owns you.

N: We celebrate the gift of air.
N brings in the chimes and moves with them
Air is invisible and all pervasive

Without air we die. It sustains every living plant and creature and sculpts every rock into strange and beautiful shapes.

All of us share the same breath. Air is the breath of life.
N, with flick of the hand, allows chimes to peel out and places them in the sacred space

N: We celebrate the gift of water.
N brings in the water
Life began in water. Science tells us that life emerged in the oceans about 4 billion years ago. Life came ashore about 650 million years ago and it brought water with it in the cells of every living creature. Our bodies are 70% water.

Water is vital. It is more precious than gold, more valuable than oil or any other mineral substance.

Water is the most potent symbol of life

N: We celebrate the gift of fire.
Fire has held mystery since the beginning of time. Fire evokes a sense of aliveness, unpredictability and sparkle. We recognise the sun, creation's source of energy and life, and are in awe of its power to warm the death of winter into spring's green life. Brigid's fire burned in Kildare for over 1500 years. It was extinguished in the 16th century and was symbolically re-lit in Kildare in 1993.

One person holds up the Brigid light for everyone to see
Each season has its own particular beauty and symbolism but spring speaks so forcefully of light, newness and rebirth. We rejoice in this newness of life as we praise and thank Our God, the giver of all life.

One of the lovely signs that spring is here, is that the days are gradually growing brighter. Light is overpowering the darkness.

We began by bringing the Brigid Light to the centre of our gathering place … the Light symbolising Christ Our Light who is the centre of our busy world. St Brigid brought light where there was darkness. We want that light to spread to the four corners of our country, to the four corners of our world or wherever the light needs to overpower the darkness. So we now light four candles from Brigid's light … and pray that the Light of Brigid will reach North – South – East and West, dispelling the darkness of wrongdoing and destruction.

Four people come forward slowly to light one candle each and they hold them for a moment facing in each of the four directions before placing them at four points in the Sacred Space

Song: Christ be Our Light[1]

PRESENTATION OF SOME OF THE QUALITIES OF BRIGID

Spring plants, which are so symbolic of new life, new beginnings and renewed hope, are carried forward to the Sacred Space, each one depicting a distinctive quality or characteristic of Brigid's life. A narrator calls out clearly each of the qualities as individuals carry forward a spring plant labelled with that named quality:
Hospitality; Compassion; Justice; Earthwoman; Peacemaker; Healer; Poet; Counsellor.

Earthwoman
Spring is here. It is time to prepare the ground for planting.

There is a folk legend which says that if the lark sings on Brigid's day then we are in for a good Spring.

Lá Fhéile Bríde, as it is called in Irish, is traditionally one of the focal points of the farming year in Ireland and the starting point of preparation for the spring sowing.

St Brigid can truly be referred to as the *Earthwoman*. She worked on the land, sowing and nurturing crops which provided for the needs of the people of Ireland of her time. She lived close to the earth and she would want us to care for the earth in our day. We too need to touch the earth with gentleness.

Song: Touch the Earth[2]

Woman of Hospitality
Many stories are told of Brigid – how people came to her when they were in great need. She gave milk, bread, fruit and vegetables and encouraged people to share what they had with their needy neighbours.

A story is told that one day a friend brought her a basket of choice apples, saying they were for Brigid and her community. The friend stood by and watched in amazement as Brigid distributed the apples to the poor people around her. 'They were for you and your sisters, not for them', her friend said, to which she replied, 'What is mine is theirs.' Can I say that?

Song: Whatsoever you do to the least of my people[3]

Peacemaker:
Brigid has been referred to, as 'Brigid, the outlaw, turning back the streams of war.' No better model could be found for peacemaking than Brigid. In the Ireland of her day feuds between various clans were common and she was often called in to settle these feuds – to make the peace.

The story of Brigid giving away her father's precious sword to a poor man saying he could exchange it for money that would help him to buy food for himself and his family, is a story that has huge significance in our world today where military spending on arms of destruction and war is in billions of dollars, while at the same time millions of human beings die of hunger and many preventable diseases. So we stand together and hold the four candles lit earlier. We turn towards the North, South, East and West praying that the streams of war can indeed be turned back.

Song: Turn Back The Streams of War[4]

Prayer said together:
You were a woman of peace.
You brought harmony where there was conflict.
You brought light to the darkness.
You brought hope to the downcast.
May the mantle of your peace cover those who are troubled and anxious,
and may peace be firmly rooted in our hearts and in our world.
Inspire us to act justly and to reverence all that God has made.
Brigid, you were a voice for the wounded and the weary, strengthen what
is weak within us.
Calm us into a quietness that heals and listens.
May we grow each day into greater wholeness in mind, body and spirit.
Amen.[5]

Woman of Compassion

Brigid was always known for her welcoming and open approach to those
who came to her. Her monastery at Kildare was noted as being a place of
hospitality and a refuge. People came to her – not just for bread, milk
and vegetables – but also because she assured them of their God-given
dignity and right to exist. She had a warm, compassionate heart that
reached out to all.

In our time, as we became more and more aware of the dreadful
plight of refugees worldwide, Brigid challenges us to reach out with a
warm, welcoming, compassionate heart to those who come to our
country seeking a better quality of life.

So, by our reflection on some of Brigid's qualities we see how she calls
us as clearly today and she did in 5th century Ireland to let our light
shine by showing forth these same characteristics or qualities in our lives.

PRESENTATION AND BLESSING OF ST BRIGID'S CROSSES

For many of us, the great association with St Brigid in Ireland is the St
Brigid's Cross. There is the custom down the centuries of making this
cross and giving it to people to place in their homes on St Brigid's day. It
is seen as a protection against fire, sickness and danger.

Distribution of Crosses to each person; they are held up for the blessing

God of all creation and Lord of Light, you have given us life and entrusted your creation to us to use it and to care for it. We now ask you to bless these crosses made from green rushes in memory of St Brigid who used the cross to recall and to teach your Son's death and resurrection. May these crosses be a sign of our sharing in the Paschal Mystery of your Son and a sign of your protection of our lives, our land and its creatures, through Brigid's intercession during the coming year and always. Through Christ our Lord. Amen.

Reflection on the Cross
As we look at the extremities of the cross, reaching as they do to the four points of the compass, let it remind us that all the peoples of the earth belong to one family under God, our Father and Mother.

As we look at the interlacing in the centre, let us understand that human survival depends on human beings of all nations learning to embrace one another, with generosity, understanding, respect, and a willingness to share the good things of the earth with justice.[6]

BLESSING WITH WATER FROM ST BRIGID'S WELL

There are many holy wells dotted around Ireland. People have gone there for centuries and still go for healing of one kind or another. St Brigid's Well in Kildare is one such place that still attracts lots of pilgrims from near and far. It is always amazing to gather there with people and to observe the faith with which they approach the well, bathing their feet, putting the water on their eyes and praying.

The container of water, placed earlier in the Sacred Space, is held by one person as participants are invited to come forward.

While we sing 'Come to the Water'. We invite you to come forward, to touch the water, bless yourself with it, take it in your hands and reflect on what it is you wish to be healed of at this time.

Song: Come to the Water[7]

I think Brigid's wish for all of us would be, the lovely old Irish prayer: 'May God give you to drink from the well that never runs dry.'

A CHOICE OF REFLECTIVE POEMS ON BRIGID

Choose one of the following poems:

13 Shouts for St Brigid
Brigid! You usher in the Spring!
Lady! New Awakenings!
Brigid! You welcome all who visit!
Lady! Hospitality!
Brigid! You guard our families and flocks!
Lady! Prosperity!
Brigid! You shelter the poor in your cloak!
Lady! The Good News!
Brigid! You inspire singers and writers!
Lady! The gift of Poetry!
Brigid! You strengthen workers in metal!
Lady! The vessels and tools!
Brigid! You guide the hands of healers!
Lady! Our precious health!
Brigid! You soften the hate that divides us!
Lady! The hope for peace!
Brigid! You cherish what comes to birth!
Lady! Home and school!
Brigid! You mirror Jesus in your life!
Lady! Love for all!
Brigid! You bless our streams and wells!
Lady! The countryside!
Brigid! You smile in sea and sky!
Lady! The world's beauty!
Brigid! You embrace us deep in your heart!
Lady! Always protected![8]

When I think of Brigid
I think of milk and the slosh of milk between buckets,
Of milk churned quietly into butter,
Of generous milk poured for the wayfarer;

I think of oatcakes and griddlecakes readied for the stranger;
I think of oatgroves
And a chapel rising from the forest;

I think of green rushes plaited into crosses;
Of fragrant turf and a fire kept longburning;

A sword melted and its opals sold to feed the hungry;

I think of the generations looking upward from their troubles
And a sheltering cloak spread warmly over the world.[9]

FINAL BLESSING

May the arms of God be about you,
The way of Christ guide you,
The strength of the Spirit support you,
And may Mary and Brigid be close to you always.

References:
1. Bernadette Farrell (CD of that title is availble. OCP Publications 1994)
2. Kathy Sherman CSJ (Tape of that name available. Also on CD 'We will Remember' by Carmel Boyle and Ger Holton, 2002)
3. Words and music: Willard F. Jabusch
4. Roy Arbuckle
5. *Solas Bhríde*, Kildare 1997
6. Celtic Reflections card, *St Brigid's Cross*, AfRI, Action From Ireland,1992
7. John B Foley SJ and OCP Publications
8. Tom Hamill, *Education for Changing Times*, Armagh, April 1999
9. Pádraig Daly OSA

Remembering Those Sitting Exams

General Comment

So often in a parish setting we express much concern about our young people not being interested in church events. When the time comes to sit important exams, such as the Junior Cert and Leaving Cert, they are usually anxious and nervous and are more open to participating in something which really is of concern to them. I believe therefore it is good to organise a short service for them. Ideally it is desirable if a small group of young people could be involved in the planning and preparation.

This could be an evening event some weeks before they actually sit the exams. Again, the creation of an atmosphere that is welcoming, warm and friendly is vital.

The advertising of the event needs to be done in various ways. One way is to ask parishioners to take invitations to young people whom they know; another is to get students themselves to issue invitations to classmates.

Welcome and Introduction

Welcome to our young people doing Junior and Leaving Certificate in June and to parents and friends who are here to surround you with their loving support and prayer.

I invite you to relax and to see this as your special time … time away from study, just to focus on how you are and on how God is with you, guiding and directing you along the journey of your life.

So to begin, we are going to bring some special symbols to this sacred space.

- A work of art done in wood – 'a boat on the sea': it symbolises tonight each one of you on the sea of life which is sometimes calm and at other times rather stormy.
- The hand holding a person carefully.. It's a symbol of the hand of God holding you carefully and safely at this time and always.
- The hand with the light, again a symbol of your hand which will be very active in putting on paper the answer to various questions … but

the light of the Holy Spirit is there with you as you do so. Trust that Light .
• Then we place some books, files and pens- a symbol of your learning, your study which takes up so much of your time.

A suitable song is sung or played, e.g. 'Gather us, O God'[1]

Scripture Reading: Matthew 6:25-34

Guided Meditation
I invite you now to relax and to enter into this quiet time … Try to relax and not be too conscious of the people around you. Just rest and be still. If it feels comfortable for you, close your eyes and listen to the music in the background … Allow your body to rest on the chair that supports you. Place your feet comfortably on the floor, getting the feeling of being in touch with the earth beneath you.
Be aware of your breathing – the fact that you breathe in and out all the time … breathing in life and energy and breathing out worries and troubles … Just relax.
I invite you now, in your imagination to go to a beautiful place in the countryside … Notice the trees, the flowers; feel the fresh warm breeze against your skin … feel the warm glow of the sunshine on your face … listen to the song of the birds around you in the trees … Rest there and relax …
Slowly become aware of a Presence there …
Jesus is in this beautiful place …
You are now in the presence of the One who formed you … who saw that you are good …. You hear Jesus call you by name: 'I call you by name … you are mine.' 'You are precious to me and I love you.' …
Talk to Jesus in the peace of this beautiful place … Tell him about your hopes and dreams for yourself … tell him about your worries, your concerns as you prepare for the important exam in the next couple of weeks. See Jesus listen very carefully to you …
Hear him reassure you that all will be well … 'Don't be afraid; I am with you.'…
Don't worry … You have special gifts … use them …

Know you are held in the palm of God's hand ... You are secure, looked upon lovingly ... God knows your inner beauty and goodness ... He is telling you now to enjoy who you are ...

So rest and relax in the presence of the One who loves you now ... Feel strength rise within you ... Be aware of your gift of courage ... Whatever troubles you, just let it go now and allow courage to turn it to good ... God is telling you now that he will be your light in darkness, your companion, your friend, your strength ... Rest in that love ...

Now begin to move back home from this beautiful spot ... Know that you bring this place and this God with you in your heart, your memory. You can revisit this place whenever you feel the need to be renewed and relaxed ...

Be aware of where you are now ... the chair on which you sit ... the floor beneath you ... the music in the background ... your breathing in and out ... the people around you ... Look around you ... Be grateful for these people and for all who have helped you and encouraged you to reach this moment ... Catch this calmness and hold it ... and may it stay with you in the days ahead and especially during the time of your exams.

Song sung or played: 'Enfold me in your Love' [2]

Movement:
Each one is invited to the sacred space to light a candle to symbolise their trust in Christ, their Light, while soft music is playing in the background.

Prayers of thanks and intercession (prepared and spontaneous)

1. God bless all our parents and friends who are doing so much to help us at this special time. Lord hear us.

2. We thank you God for all the schools and the teachers who prepare us for life through our education. Bless them all Lord. Lord hear us.

3. We ask you God tonight to be close to each of us in the days and weeks ahead as we prepare for our exams. Help us to remain calm and peaceful. Lord hear us.

4. We ask you Lord to guide us to study wisely and well. Guide us in all things. Lord hear us.

Concluding Prayer (said together)
God, we thank you for this special time we've had together. Thank you for the reassurance you give us that we are not alone but that you are with us every step of the way. Bless each one of us in the days and weeks ahead. Help us to do our best.
Thank you for our parents, teachers, friends and all who support us in so many ways.
May God's peace and love be with each of us, the Father, Son and Holy Spirit. Amen.

A closing song: Circle us, O God[3]

References
1. *A Special Collection* by Monica Brown. Monica Brown and Emmaus Productions 1997
2. CD *Quiet my Soul* by Monica Brown, Emmaus Productions 20003
3. CD *I Will Not Forget You,* NALR 1993

Mother's Day and Father's Day

General Comment

Other key moments in the life of the parish are Mother's Day and Father's Day. Society now places much emphasis on these occasions. It is very important, I believe, to also use these occasions in church to thank God for our parents and to ask God's continued blessing on them.

It's an occasion to reflect on the very special vocation of parenting. It calls for great sensitivity, given the fact that some people have a very negative experience of 'father' or 'mother' and others may be childless or have lost a child.

We aim to be as inclusive as possible by looking on the mothering and fathering role as something done by many in the community in the way they reach out and care for others in their day-to-day lives.

In the prayers of intercession, prayers are included for all – those experiencing difficulty in parental relationships, those remembering parents who have died and so on. It's a question of incorporating Mother's Day and Father's Day into the regular Sunday liturgy.

- At the welcome and introduction, they (mothers/fathers) are especially welcomed.
- At the homily time something special can be said. On one occasion we invited three mothers of differing age groups to share something of how they experienced motherhood as a vocation and it was very successful in that it captured people's attention in a very real way.
- At the prayers of intercession, special prayers are included for mothers (fathers) living and dead, for those experiencing difficulty in relationships, those who are childless and those who have died.
- After Holy Communion and before the final blessing mothers (fathers) are invited to stand and the congregation extends their hands in blessing towards mothers (fathers) as a special blessing prayer is said. They are then given a flower (or scroll) by some of the children present. Some sample scroll prayers are included below.

Blessing Prayer for Father's Day
Blessed are you, God of all life.
You have given to us the gift of the father of our family.
Today, we honour him and we thank God, Our Father,
for the many things that are ours because of him.

His love for us is a sign of your great love for all people.
Bless him today with your strength and power
so that he can continue to show love in our family.

May we, as a family help him in his duties as a parent
by showing respect, obedience and deep affection.

Bless him, Lord, with happiness and good health,
with peace and joy.

This blessing, we pray,
come down, on the father of our family,
in the name of the Father,
and of the Son,
and of the Holy Spirit. Amen.

When God Created Fathers,
He thought of love and care,
Encouraging and helpful words,
Kind and caring deeds,
Love and trust and thoughtfulness –
The kind a family needs;
A patient heart, a helping hand,
warmth and wisdom.
Thank God for fathers
Who are more than good.
They share so much of what they have,
To make us feel so good.

Mother's Day Prayer
God, our Loving Father,
You compare your own love for your people
with the love of a mother for her children.
Look with kindness on these mothers here today;
Bless and reward them for their motherly care;
Give them comfort in moments of sorrow
and joy in their work for their families.
Listen to their prayers and
bless them in all they do for us;
Bless them with joy, love, laughter and pride in their family
and surround them with many good friends.
This blessing we ask for
the mother of each family,
in the name of the Father,
Son and of the Holy Spirit.
Amen.

The following piece can be made into a Scroll for each mother present:

What is a Mother?
A mother is someone who cares about you …
She's someone you could always run to as a child …
Someone you can always turn to as you grow …
Whatever the situation, a mother seems to know just what you need …
And whatever the need, she's willing to help, ready to listen, able to understand.
She's someone who encourages you to be all you can be – yet accepts you just as you are.
A mother is someone who will always have a special place in your heart and your life …
especially when she's a wonderful mother like you …

Grandparent's Day, 26 July

General Comment

In recent years we have been celebrating Grandparent's Day in the parish on 26 July which is the feast of St Joachim and St Anne, the parents of Mary and the grandparents of Jesus. In our community, grandparents play a pivotal role in the lives of their grandchildren and so we see it as very important to acknowledge and to celebrate their special gift in the family.

This occasion is publicised in advance through the parish bulletin. We encourage grandparents to attend the regular morning Mass.

At this Mass they are especially welcomed; they are invited to reflect on their role as grandparents, just as Joachim and Anne were in the life of Jesus.

Special prayers are included in the Intercessions for grandparents and then a prayer of blessing is said as all extend hands towards them.

After the blessing some appropriate reflection, made into a scroll, is presented to each one.

The cup of tea and chat afterwards is a way of continuing to celebrate their presence.

A Blessing for Grandparents

Lord of Life, we are grateful for the gift of these grandparents.
You have chosen them and brought them to this day..
They have shared with their families
life and wisdom and many gifts and talents.
Our parents brought us into life;
in our grandparents we have sensed and felt
our history that lies at the heart of our family.
We ask that those who guided our early steps
and called forth our hidden talents,
may be richly rewarded by you, O God.
May all grandparents be blessed today by your faithful love
and kept safe by your grace and protection. Amen

Prayers of Intercession
1. We pray today for the grandparents in our community that they will be generous in sharing their wisdom, knowledge and experience of human life with us all.
Lord hear us.

2. We ask you, God, to reward all grandparents who are so important in the lives of their families. Be close to them always.
Lord hear us.

3. We pray for all grandchildren that they will come to understand the wisdom of their grandparents and respond with honour and respect.
Lord hear us.

4. We pray for all our grandparents who have died. Give them, Lord, the happiness and peace of your heavenly home.
Lord hear us.

In order to create a Scroll that can be presented to each grandparent, invite children to do a brainstorm on the importance of their grandparents in their lives. Their responses will then be woven together to create an attractive Scroll.
Something similar can be done to create a suitable Scroll for Mother's Day and Father's Day.

Blessing of Expectant Parents

General Comment

A significant time in the life of any couple is when a baby is conceived. There is a mixture of feelings, from excitement to hope, to anxiety, to apprehension when a couple becomes aware of the pregnancy. It is a sacred moment and one which we as a church community need to acknowledge and ritualise in some way. Some older women have shared with us how they, in the past, asked the priest to bless them in their pregnancy. This was seen as a private event. For a number of years we, in our parish, have been having a special service of blessing for expectant mothers or couples. We usually have it four times yearly to coincide with the four seasons: winter, spring, summer and autumn.

It is important to spread the news of the Blessing in as many ways as possible. We find it is good to place a poster in the parents' room of the -local schools, at the health centre, at the local post office or wherever young parents are likely to be. The parish bulletin alone is not likely to reach a significant number.

The creation of the space where the blessing will take place is important. The main part of the church is not a suitable venue because it is too large for a small gathering. A room off the church or a hall can be more easily adapted so that seating is in a circle and a sacred space is created with cloths, candles and other appropriate symbols. It is our experience over the years that people who come for this blessing are touched deeply by it. They are always very pleased that this special time in their lives is acknowledged to be sacred and they are helped to continue to reflect on God-with-them in and through each moment of their lives and especially now as they carry new life within the womb.

Introduction

The beginning of new life is exciting for you and for your family. However, it can also be an anxious time because you worry if the child will be all right. You make many plans; you share many hopes and dreams for this little one. But above all you hope and pray that the baby will grow safe and well. So this little gathering is saying to you, 'Yes, we all believe this is a precious, sacred time in your lives.' You trust in God that God will give you all you need to ensure that your child will be healthy and that you will have a safe delivery. So, as a faith community we gather to support you and to bless you at this significant time in your life.

Song: Spirit of the Living God[1]

Scripture: Isaiah 49:14-16 'Can a mother forget her infant ... I will never forget you.'

Placing of symbols on the sacred space: Each parent lights a floating candle and places it on water ... a symbol of the new life they carry within them.

Psalm 139: The All-knowing and Ever-present God.

Prayer

Dear Lord, I know that you care for me and understand how I feel.
You have always surrounded me with your love.
Help me to surround with love this new life.
I depend on you, Lord, now more than ever.
Stay close to me in the days that lie ahead.
Bless the preparations for the birth of this baby.
In any uncertainty and doubt, strengthen and reassure me
so that I may always reflect your love.
Amen.

Song: Circle us O God[2]

Psalm during pregnancy (said together):
I realised at once that something new had happened;
    a tiny flutter of awareness.
I am now not I, but we; someone's deep within me,
    part of me but not me.
O God, Giver of all life, I am in awe at this new life within me
    and I pray for the grace to carry it well,
    to honour the rhythms and seasons of the birthing cycle.
May I be patient with the morning sickness
    that comes to me even at sunset
and the inner dance that keeps me awake through half-sleepless nights.

May I celebrate this season of change
    and the energy to provide for the needs of this growing life within me
    that these changes make possible.

Help me to wait patiently, especially at those times
    when I wish that I could just take a peek inside
    to find out who this little person is
    who is tap-dancing on my ribs while I try to sleep.

I want so much to be a good mother,
    to care for and nourish this new life.
Help me to gift this child with all the love I can,
    during this time of pregnancy
    and also when my baby is born into fuller life.

O God, help me, for I am nervous;
    I do not feel ready for this awesome task.
Free me from my fear of a painful delivery;
    may it be a holy and blessed experience for us both.

Free me from my fear of inadequacy
    about raising this child into maturity and holiness.
Please help me, O God, to protect my child who is yours as well.[3]

Guided Reflection

Be quiet and still … Rest and relax into this moment … the present …
Hear God speak to your heart this evening, 'Be still and know I am your
God' …
Journey to the inner core of your being … to be with God …
In God's presence allow your deeper thoughts and feelings to come to the
surface …
How are you feeling about your pregnancy? … talk to God about this …
Hear God reassure you that your baby is alive within you … this baby is
precious, unique, very special …
Be aware of the privilege which is yours to carry this precious new life
within you … This baby is totally dependent on you … Again hear God
tell you that you are not alone in this: 'Don't be afraid or anxious or wor-
ried, I am with you … I hold you and your baby in the palm of my
hand. Rest and relax in my love.

In the quietness of your heart express thanks to God for this baby you're
carrying … Tell God of your dreams and your hopes for this child …
Thank God for all those around you who are supporting you through
your pregnancy and looking forward with you to the birth …

Allow any other thoughts or feelings you may have now to surface …
Share them with God who loves you and wants what is best for you …
'Yes, be still and know I am your God.'

Our Lady, the inspiration for all mothers

Song: When Creation Was Begun[4]

Litany

Jesus, Lord and Saviour, from the cross you gave us your mother, Mary,
as an example to imitate, as a disciple to follow, as a mother to intercede
for us. Let us now remember, Mary, a woman who struggled with life yet
remained faithful to the God who called her. We ask her to stand with us
in our lives as mother, sister and friend.

Mary, young girl on the threshold of womanhood, Stand with us.
Mary, fiancée of Joseph, Stand with us.
Mary, facing an unexpected pregnancy, Stand with us.
Mary, young married woman, Stand with us.
Mary, heavily pregnant, Stand with us.
Mary, suffering the pains of childbirth, Stand with us.
Mary, in the joy of holding a healthy baby, Stand with us.
Mary, woman of faith and hope, Stand with us.
Mary, woman of strength and power, Stand with us.
Mary, daughter, mother, sister, friend, Stand with us.

A Blessing Prayer for Mothers
O Lord of all life, hear our prayer as we ask your blessing upon these
mothers who have been given the gift of life to bear within their bodies.
We rejoice in this gift and pray that the children alive within these mothers
may soon join us, in the light of day. May these children be healthy in
body and mind and free of physical difficulties. Give these mothers,
peace of mind and health of body as they care for the new life within
them. Grant that when the time comes they may have a safe delivery.
Look over these expectant mothers and fathers as they look forward to
the birth of this child.
We pray now in silence for these mothers, fathers and babies.
Pause for silent prayer

Blessing of Oil and Anointing of Mothers
Lord God almighty,
We ask you to bless and make holy this oil which you have created.
Let this oil protect and bring health in body and mind to all who use it
and especially the expectant parents here this evening.
May we be filled with your blessings and give thanks to you,
the living and true God, through Christ our Lord. Amen.

Each one is blessed with thee words:
Through this oil of anointing may God bless and strengthen you during
your pregnancy. May you and your baby be healthy and strong and may
you be blessed with a safe delivery.

Final Blessing

May the mother of our Lord Jesus, Mary, all the saints, all holy women and the mothers of the past, be with you.

May the strength of God help you to carry your child so that when the time finally arrives, these children of God will be born into the world wrapped in love, joy and peace.

May the blessing of God, compassionate as a mother, of God the Son and the Holy Spirit rest upon you and upon your children. Amen.

References
1. Words and music: Michael Iverson
2. *I Will Never Forget You,* Volume 2, Carey Landry
3. Adapted from *Prayers for a Planetary Pilgrim* by Edward Hays 1989
4. Words: J.P. Lecot; Music:Paul Decha, Kevin Mayhew Ltd

For parents who have had a child baptised during the year

Welcome and introduction

We welcome each one of you here today as you come to give thanks for the child born into your family during the past year. On the occasion of your baby's baptism you publicly proclaimed that you wanted that child to belong to the faith community of the parish. So today, with so many families here, we truly celebrate that great sense of belonging to an extended family and together you express again your deep gratitude for that blessing of new life among you.

Invitation to light a night light for the child/family

Opening song: 'This Child of Ours'[1]

Opening prayer

O God, you gather us today as one family in this parish community. We come to give you thanks, God, for the gift and blessing of our children in our lives. May we always be truly thankful. Help us to continue to nourish these children's lives by our care, commitment and good example. We pray that we will always be aware, God, that you are the source of all life and goodness. We make this prayer through Christ our Lord

Scripture: Matthew 19:13-15

'Let the children come to me and do not prevent them.'

Guided Reflection (with suitable background music)

Be quiet ... let go of the day's busyness ... just be ... rest ... this is time for you ... let go gently if you can and allow yourself to be lead in the next few minutes ... make yourself comfortable ... notice your breathing ... and relax ... slowly enter into the inner room of your heart where you can be alone with yourself and your God.

I'm going to bring you back in time ... back to the time your baby was conceived ... when you found out you were pregnant ... when the pregnancy was confirmed ... What was that like for you? ... a happy, exciting time ... or maybe a fearful, anxious time ... Was there surprise, delight, shock? ... Who did you tell? ... What was the time of pregnancy like for you? ... Did you feel well or were there times when you felt really unwell?

The birth of the baby ... a time to remember too ... seeing your baby for the first time ... recall that time now ... the excitement ...maybe the awareness of the responsibility now placed on you ... Your decision to have the baby baptised as a Catholic ... why did you decide on that? ... Entering the baby's name ... the visit to your home of the baptism faith friend, attending the meeting with other parents who were also preparing to have their baby baptised ... Recall now the day you brought the baby to church for the baptism ... what was that like for you? ... What do you remember of the ceremony? ... your baby was welcomed into the Christian community as a child of God ... What has it been like for you since? ... The milestones reached by the child ... the smiles ... the gestures ... the great affection ... the screams ... cries ... losing nights' sleep ... How has the arrival of this baby affected your relationship with your partner, with other family members? See that baby now in your mind's eye ... what are the things you really hope for, for this child? ... If you could talk to your child at this moment what might you say? ... Offer that child to God now ... invite God to surround him/her with love, peace and joy ... Hear God say to you now, 'Your baby is precious to me and I love him/her' ... 'I hold that baby in the palm of my hand' ... What is it you want God to do for you so that you can give that child all the love and care he/she deserves? ... Tell God now ... maybe you have fears ... talk to him about it ... hear Him say to you, 'Don't be afraid, I am with you ... I will be with you in all your joys and sorrows, rest in my love' ...

Now slowly begin to come back to this place ... notice your breathing ... the seat on which you are sitting ... be aware of the people around you ... focus on the candle at the centre ...

An invitation to share after the meditation, perhaps a prayer of thanks

Pass out a little card and invite people to jot down a word or sentence expressing what they hope for their child as he/she grows and develops.

Proceed to central sacred space and place the card there near their lighted night lights while a song is played or sung.

Song: 'You are a Miracle'[2]

A Prayer of Blessing said over these cards:
God bless each family here as they place their hopes and dreams for their children before you. Give each one the strength they need in their role as parents. May each one continue to help their children to be aware that they are embraced by your love, God, all through their lives. We make this prayer through Christ, our Lord. Amen.

References
1. David Haas, on CD *Throughout All Time*, GIA Publications 1997
2. Monica Brown, CD *God Delights in You*, Emmaus Productions 2001

A Service for Parents when Children Begin School

General Comment
The time a child starts going to school is a very significant moment in the life of a parent. It too is a sacred moment of letting go and entrusting the child to others for extended periods of time.

I believe it is a time for the parish to touch into the experience of parents and to help them to reflect in a prayerful way on this step in their lives and in the life of their child. In many cases parents tend to stay on in the school building during the first days, as the little ones are settling in. So it is an ideal occasion to invite them to participate in a short prayerful gathering that will help to focus them on their experience of letting go and where God is in that.

I find they are very happy to have this time together for some prayerful reflection. It is an opportunity not to be missed for making contact with young parents.

Gather in the Parent's Room (while they wait to pick up the little ones during the first days)

Create the atmosphere:
A space with lights … the central light for Christ who is at the centre of everything. In the space have some childrens' toys and books.

Welcome and Introduction (with some background music)
Welcome to each one as we take a little time now to reflect on this special moment in your lives and in the life of your child as he/she begins school. It's another big step in that child's life and a very significant moment for you as you begin to let go of this little one and entrust him/her to the care of the school. We take this time to acknowledge your own feelings and to become aware of God with you and your little ones at this important time in your lives.

Invite parents to light a candle, naming their child and maybe sharing their reason for giving the child that name.

Scripture: Matthew 19:13-15, 'Let the children come...' *or*
Isaiah. 49:15-18, 'Can a mother forget her child ...'

Song: Isaiah 49[1]

Guided Meditation
Some elements of the meditation in the ritual on pages 36/37 could be used on this occasion; perhaps recalling the birth of the child, the christening and the stages that have brought him/her to this day; how they feel in the letting-go as their child takes another step by starting school ... Asking Jesus to be with the child, teacher and the family at this time.

After the Guided Meditation:
Invite parents to share a word or sentence expressing their feelings at this time as they let go of the little ones into school life.

Reflection: 'Speak To Us of Children'[2]

Concluding Prayer (said together)
We thank you, God, for this time together today. We thank and praise you for our children and we ask you to bless them now as they begin life at school. Help us to let go of them in a spirit of trust, knowing that they continue to be helped to discover and use their individual gifts in the school environment. Guide their teachers in the awesome task which is theirs in helping to nourish the overall development of these, our children. We ask this now through Christ Our Lord. Amen.

Closing Song: : This Child of Ours[3]

References
1. Carey Landry and NALR 1975
2. *The Prophet,* Kahil Gibran
3. David Haas; On CD *Throughout All Time,* GIA Publications 1997

Affirmation and Blessing of our Teachers

General Comment

The teachers in our local schools do a wonderful job. Theirs is truly a vocation and one that calls for our ongoing support in the parish. For a number of years we have gathered the teachers of our three schools together in early October for a short service whereby they are affirmed and helped to reflect on their special vocation, and are blessed and sent forth for another school year. We arrange this on an afternoon which they have set aside for a staff meeting so as to minimise disruption to the regular school schedule.

Invariably, the response to this gathering is extremely positive. Teachers acknowledge the value of having time to step off the merry-go-round of school life just to be together, to pause, to reflect and pray. It is facilitated by members of the parish team.

On this occasion we arrange a special afternoon tea whereby they have the opportunity to interact with staff of the various schools. It also builds a bond between school and parish which is vitally important for the life of the community.

Welcome and Introductory words

We happily welcome each one of you to this gathering today. You, the teachers in our schools, play such a significant role in the lives of the children. This time together now is an opportunity to reflect on the very privileged ministry of yours and a time to ask God's blessing on you, on the children whom you teach and on their families. In a very real sense, you are co-creators with God in the task of helping children to reach their full potential.

Lighting of Candles

So, we invite a teacher from each school to light a candle – a symbol of Christ, the Light of our lives, which is reflected by each school and each member of staff.

Gathering Song: 'Gather Us O God'[1]

41

Reading:
One thing stirs me when I look back at my youthful days: it is the fact that so many people gave me something or were something to me without knowing it. Such people had a decisive influence on me; they entered into my life and became powers within me. Much that I should not otherwise have felt clearly, or done so effectively, was felt or done as it was, because I stand, as it were, under the sway of these people. Hence I always think that we all live spiritually by what others have given us in the significant hours of life. If we had before us those who have thus been a blessing to us and could tell them how it came about, they would be amazed to learn what passed over from their life to ours.[2]

Guided Reflection (Soft music playing in the background)
(Using the Acorn as a symbol):
Hold the acorn in your hands ... small ... fragile
See it as a symbol of each child in your class ... your school ...

Within that acorn is much potential for growth and life ... that growth and flourishing can only happen if the environment is favourable ... good soil, heat, moisture, nourishment, tender care.

Everett, the 18th century poet, says 'Tall oaks from little acorns grow.' Become aware of the privilege that is yours ... helping to create the conditions so that the children with you can reach their full potential.

Reflect for a moment on your own life, your own nurturing and nourishing that brought out what is best in you ... that brought you to where you are today ... Take a moment to delight in who you are ... in what you are about ... savour with delight the privilege that is yours in being part of something so awesome, so great ... creating in your classroom ... an atmosphere where each little one is treasured and affirmed, where you are able to bring him/her to a sense of their own preciousness, their own uniqueness ... by touching into what is deep within each one ...

Just as the one who plants the acorn and tends it will probably never live to see the mighty oak ... so too you don't always see the end product for what you are about each day ... But, 'What may not be for us may be hopefully because of us.'

In order for the oak to grow strong it grows slowly and demands much patient waiting and sometimes much frustration. So too, what you do calls for endless patience ... endless staying power...

42

Notice again the care and gentleness with which you are holding that acorn ... Hear God say to you in the quietness of this prayer time: 'I am holding you carefully and tenderly in the palm of my hand.' ... You too are privileged to hold and to care for the little ones I place in your care ...you are called to say 'yes' that the whisper of God might be heard through all the noise in each child's life ...

So the acorn in your hand contains all the possibility for fullness of life ... Lord, as we look into the branches of the oak we know that it grows great and strong because it grows slowly and well.

Help us to keep this in mind as we work day to day with each child in our care.

Song: St Teresa's Prayer, 'Christ Has No Body Now But Yours'[3]

Reflection:
It helps now and then to step back and take the long view.
The Kingdom is not only beyond our efforts;
   it is even beyond our vision.
We accomplish in our lifetime only a tiny fraction
   of the magnificent enterprise that is God's work.
Nothing we do is complete, which is another way of saying
   that the Kingdom always lies beyond us.
No statement says all that could be said.
No prayer fully expresses our faith.
No confession brings wholeness.
No programme accomplishes fully the mission.
No set of goals and objectives includes everything.
This is what we are about.
We plant the seeds that one day will grow.
We water seeds already planted knowing that they hold future promise.
We lay foundations that will need further development.
We provide yeast that produces effects far beyond our capabilities.
We cannot do everything
   and there is a sense of liberation in realising that.
This enables us to do something and to do it very well.
It may be incomplete, but it is a beginning, a step along the way,

an opportunity for the Lord's grace to enter and do the rest.
We may never see the end results
    but that is the difference between the master builder and the worker.
We are workers, not master builders; ministers, not messiahs.
We are prophets of a future not our own.
Amen.[4]

Quiet time for personal reflection:

Song: Here I am Lord[5]

Reflection
In an old Chinese story a wise teacher asks his students to identify the
most satisfying thing in life. There were many good answers given such as
'a happy marriage', 'good health' and 'close friends'. But the sage said they
had all failed to give the correct answer. 'The most satisfying thing in
life', he said, 'is to see a child confidently walk down the road on their
own after you have shown them the way to go.'

Litany of Intercession
Response: Lord God, we thank you.
1. For the talents and the abundance of gifts that are ours …
2. For the children in our classrooms who are precious and unique…
3. For the families in this community whom we have come to know over
the years…
4. For all who work within our schools, in the community and in the
parish to bring light and hope to those we meet …
5. For the times when your goodness has made a difference through us…

Closing Prayer
Lord, help me to make of my classroom a place where love and learning
come to life. Guide me in all that I do that I may strive, not so much to
teach as to awaken, not so much to instruct as to inspire.
Above all, help me to give my students love, a love gentle enough to
touch, but firm enough to leave them room to grow, and help me to give
it now that they may share it with a world in need of such love. I
promise this, knowing that my own life pattern is for from perfect. So I

make this commitment relying on you, Lord, and on all who are working in the schools to build your kingdom.
Stay with us and help us weave your love into the lives of the children here in this parish and allow them to do the same for us.
Through Christ our Lord. Amen.

References
1. Carey Landry, *I Will Never Forget You,* Vol 1, NALR 1993
2. *Memories of Childhood and Youth,* by Albert Schweitzer
3. John Michael Talbot, Birdwing Music 1987
4. Oscar Romero
5. Dan Schutte SJ and NALR 1981

Hope in the Face of Suicide

General Comment
'Come to me you who are heavily burdened and I will give you rest.'
Sadly, many communities are greatly affected by the incidence of death
by suicide. While the trauma is felt most deeply by the immediate family,
the friends and neighbours are also traumatised and are also searching for
answers to their constant questions: Why? How? What if?

The challenge therefore is put to the parish community to offer a
service whereby the people can come together to pray, to reflect, to
remember and to find a word that touches them with hope.

The community needs to know and to experience that 'The Lord is
close to the broken hearted.' This service tries to bring some light to the
darkness and some hope to the despairing. The planning and carrying
out of such a service calls for great sensitivity.

Invitations to the gathering are sent to individual families and friends
directly affected, but we also need to promote the event as
something which concerns all of us in the faith community who
gather in solidarity and in prayerful support.

Notices are placed in areas where the public generally can see them.

Gathering Song: Where Healing Can Begin[1]

Welcome and Introduction:
We welcome each one who has come to our Service of Hope in the Face
of Suicide. As we gather we are very much aware of the pain of grief and
loss felt by so many here. Words cannot describe or indeed capture the
depth of feeling around this issue. In each one here there are possibly
feelings of anger, guilt, anxiety and hopelessness. Suicide is a huge human
tragedy and leaves families and friends devastated. It is with the love and
support of those around you and your deep faith in God that you can
manage to go on.

Tonight we gather, then, in faith and great love, to support each other
by our presence, our prayer and our search for hope. We do trust that the
light of hope shines deeply in each one's heart, even in the darkest times.

Opening Prayer
Lord our God, we gather this day to remember loved ones whose lives
ended so suddenly and tragically. We know, God, that you are always
faithful and quick to show mercy. You are with us now in our pain and
loss. We pray for our loved ones who were suddenly taken from us.
Come to us now and comfort us with your peace and strength. We make
this prayer through Christ Our Lord. Amen.

Song: The Clouds Veil[2]

Some quiet reflective music
A scripture dialogue:

V. 1   Out of the depths of despair I cry to you, O God. Hear the
       voice of my pleading …

V.2   When you call to me … when you come to plead with me I
       listen to you …

V.1   O Lord, my God, I cry to you by day … Let my prayer come to
       you for I cry to you for help…

V.2   Don't be afraid; I am with you to help you…

V.1   I am overcome by my troubles, my heart is in anguish within
       me …

V.2   I, the Lord, am close to the broken hearted … I will heal your
       wounds …Cast all your burdens on me, your God and I will
       support you …

V.1   For me, there is no calm, no peace; whatever I dread, befalls me

V.2   I know the plans I have in mind for you; plans for peace, not
       disaster, reserving a future full of hope for you.

V.1   Hope in God! I will again praise my Saviour and my God.

or

Psalm 130
Out of the depths I cry to you, O Lord.
Lord, hear my voice!
Let your ears be attentive to my pleading!

If you, O Lord, should mark our failings,
Lord, who could stand?
But there is forgiveness with you so that you may be revered.

I wait for the Lord, my soul waits and in his Word I hope.
My soul waits for the Lord more than those
who watch for the morning.

O let us hope in the Lord!
For with the Lord there is steadfast love,
And with him is great power to redeem.
It is he who will save us from all our frailties.

Movement
*Lighting of candles to remember loved ones and, on their return to their seats,
all bless themselves with salted water as a symbol of the tears of pain and
grief.*

Reflection
Father, I come before you in my brokenness and grief. I feel so alone, so
bereft, so torn. Where are you, Lord? Yes, I can see you now, Lord. You
must be present in that person who is sitting beside me, who has sat with
me so often … she is listening. Lord, don't let her tire of me telling my
story over and over again. You see she has suffered like you and like me
… she understands.

But tomorrow Lord, will you be gone again? No, you will be that man
who has sat beside me so many times. I felt your presence Lord, when he
put his arms around me while tears of sadness, frustration and loneliness
poured down my face. He said it's alright to cry and, Jesus, it must be,
because you too cried when the widow of Naim lost her son and again
when your friend Lazarus died. Now I know that I am not crying alone.

Scripture
Mark 15:33-37 'At noon darkness came over the whole land …'

A Personal Testimony
If I wait to articulate fully my story, it will never happen. So I will start
with what I am most aware of – the pain and rawness in my heart.

Just over a year ago my brother committed suicide.

Words cannot adequately describe the hurt, the pain, the confusion and fall out from this.

I had read articles, heard programmes on the radio about suicide and always felt a sense of pain for the people and wondered how they coped. Now I know.

There are no answers, there are no solutions and the 'if only's' are great. In its own insidious way, it splits families and I think it has split our own family. We have all been hurt in different ways and on different levels and have retreated into our own corners for protection. We have discussed it for many hours, days, weeks, but maybe not saying what is really in our hearts, for fear of adding to each other's unfathomable grief.

For myself, I will never again be the same. I find that I now live on the periphery of life and have become detached from people and issues. Nothing seems important anymore. There is no rationale to my life. I wonder if I will ever really be happy again and look forward to each new day with enthusiasm as was my wont. It is not right for people to be unhappy as it is the axle of life.

We looked on helplessly, it seemed and watched him suffer intolerable mental torment and yet I know in my heart of hearts that as a family we gave him our all. This isn't any consolation; in fact it hurts all the more to know that nothing could sustain him. No amount of love, care, reassurance or help mattered in the end.

His last few hours are unknown to us. We searched all evening, late into the night and resumed the search early next morning, hoping against all the odds that we would find him safe.

Unless you have experienced the search for a missing person, you cannot understand the fear, tension, inadequacy, concern and awful feeling of hopelessness – not knowing where to start and all the time hoping your search will lead to him. As each hour passed our sadness increased and our hope faded slowly into despair. It exposed the desperate fragility of humanity and the utter unpredictability of life.

For him his pain was too much. He felt a burden on all of us so suicide seemed the obvious solution, and for him it probably was.

I doubt that he would have made a full recovery. We would never again know the brother that loved and embraced life with such passion.

His suicide was so indicative of the depth of his illness, because he was a man who loved and trusted his God implicitly. He had high moral and religious standards. This decision was so alien to him that I can only tell myself that the brother I once knew was long gone from us.

Time goes by and people get back to their lives and assume you are doing fine. It's easier to agree in most cases, but his memory and the manner of his death will be with me until the day I die. He is my first thought in the morning and last thing at night. He is constantly present with me during the day and always I ask myself 'why?' It is, in my opinion, one of the worst, or *the* worst tragedy to hit a family. Death is always a mystery, but death by suicide is absolutely incomprehensible. I have lost the joy of living. Mechanically I go through the day. I meet my friends, have innocuous conversation, fill my leisure time and when I least expect it this overwhelming wave of sadness and weariness engulfs me. It is as if someone is squeezing the life out of me. It leaves me breathless and afraid. When the sun is shining and I feel its warmth on my body, I want him to feel it too. The bluest of skies are tinged with grey for me. I cannot erase the look of pain and terror that had become his face. The awful pleading in his eyes, asking for help and relief from his great suffering – all of which seemed to be beyond our capabilities. We can no longer reach out and touch the man that was a quintessential part of our lives. We will love him a place that has no time and no space. I hope he feels none of the pain in his world that we feel here. I believe in my head that he is at peace, but it doesn't make any difference to the gut feeling. Peace is what I wish for him, because it is something that constantly seems to elude me. All I ask is that he not be judged on how he ended his life, but how he lived it and how I know that the day we buried him was not the worst day – it was all the days that followed. There is no closed chapter on death by suicide.[3]

Song: Be Not Afraid[4]

Blessing and anointing of those bereaved (For inner peace and healing)
Song: Lay Your Hands Gently Upon Us[5] *is played or sung during the anointing*

Prayers of Intercession
For everyone here
Lord, we thank you for everyone who has come here tonight and for the courage which has brought us together to share our sorrow.
Lord, hear us.

For the families affected by suicide
Father, we pray for all family members – young and old – who have lost loved ones by suicide. Lord, carry all of them through their journey of grief in all its heartbreak and give them hope.
Lord, hear us.

For friends and colleagues
Father in heaven, friend to all, full of compassion and love for those who mourn, we ask you to enfold in your loving arms those who grieve the loss of a friend or colleague through suicide. Heal and comfort them. Fill the void with your presence and keep them in your care.
Lord, hear us.

For those who have died
We pray for our loved ones whose lives ended so tragically. We also remember with joy the many good times and the laughter we shared with them. There is a saying which goes, 'God gives us our memories so we can have roses in December.' We thank you for those memories and those times and pray that those for whom we grieve this evening have completed their journey and are happy forever now in God's loving care.
Lord, hear us.

For those contemplating suicide
We pray tonight for all who are lost in their unhappy worlds and who feel just now that life is not worth living. May they find the support and help they need in God and in their communities and be enabled to live life to the full.
Lord, hear us.

A Litany of Remembrance
In the rising of the sun and in its going down, we remember them.
In the blowing of the wind and in the chill of winter, we remember them.

In the blueness of the sky and in the warmth of summer, we remember them.
In the rustling of the leaves and in the beauty of autumn, we remember them.
In the beginning of the year and when it ends, we remember them.
When we are lost and sick at heart, we remember them.
When we have joys we yearn to share, we remember them.
So long as we live, they too shall live, for they are part of us and we remember them.

Final Blessing
May the Lord bless you and keep you.
May his face shine upon you.
May he be gracious to you.
May he look upon you with kindnes.
May you know his peace.

Closing song: Isaiah 49[6]

References
1. Carey Landry and NALR 1993, *I will not forget you,* volume 2
2. Text and music by Liam Lawton, arr by John McCann, GIA publications 1998
3. Nora Prendergast *(used with permission)*
4. Bob Dufford SJ and OCP Publications 1975
5. Words and music, Carey Landry on CD *Abba Father*
6. Carey Landry & NALR 1975

Remembering our loved ones who have died
(A Service of Light in November)

General Comment
This gathering is a very significant one in the life of any parish and needs to be celebrated as such.

It is at times of death and bereavement that we really touch into people's lives and help to assure them of our support and care.

This gathering is prepared by a group of people, e.g. The Bethany Support Group with the liturgy and music groups and the parish team.

An invitation is brought to the home of each family bereaved in the previous year. This is done by the Bethany Group and it provides an ideal opportunity for a parish representative to re-connect with the bereaved families.

On the evening of the service, each family is welcomed at the entrance to the church. Again, the decoration, lighting and heating of the gathering place is very important so that people capture something of the specialness of this ritual for them.

The service can be celebrated in the context of Eucharist or it can stand alone as a service, especially if there is no priest available.

Either way people need to know that their loved ones are specially remembered by the community and that they, in their grief and loss, are surrounded by a prayerful community of people.

Welcome
As people enter the church they are welcomed by the Bethany Group. Each person receives a symbol, the words of songs to be used and a candle.

Opening song: Where Healing Can Begin[1]
or Christ Be Our Light[2]

Introduction
You are all very welcome to this special Service of Light for our loved ones who have died, for those we have had the privilege of knowing and loving as we shared our lives with them.

We are gathered here to remember a mother, a father, a husband, a wife, a grandfather or grandmother, a son or daughter, a brother or sister, a friend.

The cherished memories that we have of them can never fade because we carry what they meant to us deep in our hearts. We each have our own personal memories. We now take a few moments to recall these memories, the happy and the sad.

Everyone loves to be remembered. If we want to be remembered we have a duty to remember. Memory is a powerful thing. It keeps the past alive.

Those we remember never die. So let us spend time now with our memories of the loved ones we have lost.

Pause

I now invite ... to light the Paschal Candle, the symbol of the Risen Christ among us.
The lighted candle reminds us that in our grief and dark moments Christ our Light is with us. Our own faith tells us that those who have gone before us are now at home with Christ forever. It also assures us that we will be reunited with them again when there will be no more partings.

Song: We Will Remember[3]

Scripture readings: Wisdom 3:1-9; Thessalonians 4:13-18; John 14:1-7

Song: There is a Place[4]

Guided Reflection (Choose 1 or 2)
Reflection 1
In the quiet of this evening I invite you to be still and relax ... Try to let go of the busyness of the day and all the activities that made up your day ... and relax ... Be aware of the music in the background ... if you feel comfortable doing so, close your eyes gently ... take these few moments to be with your thoughts and feelings tonight ...

Holding in your hand the flower you've brought or which you received on your way in ... you might like to smell it, feel it, notice its shape, its colour, the many petals on it ... Tonight the flower you are holding is a symbol of your memories, your love of the person you are remembering here especially at this service ... In your mind's eye now see that person ... name him or her to yourself ... what are the qualities ... the special gifts you admired in this loved one? ... How did the person influence your life? ... Allow the special memories of this person to come to your mind ... happy memories ... sad memories ... good or not so good ... things you shared ... what you did together ... places you've been ... friends you've shared together ...

See in each petal of the flower you are holding a symbol of the memories you now recall and want to treasure ... As you hold that flower so gently and carefully, so too God is holding you and your loved one gently and carefully in his hands ...

Perhaps there is something you want to say to this person now, that you haven't had a chance to say ... do so in the quietness of your heart ... Maybe there's something that person wants to say to you? ... What might that be? ... Listen in the silence of your heart ...

Now hold these memories of your love ones out to Jesus, your friend and healer ... Pour out your feelings of sorrow and sadness ... Ask God to enter into the deep pain that's in your life at this time.

Visualise Jesus welcoming you and comforting you ... See Jesus take your memories, your feelings very gently ... Hear him reassuring you that he does care about you ... that he does understand your deep feeling of loss ... He is reassuring you that your loved one is now at peace with him ... is now welcomed home fully to God ... See in your mind's eye that person being at rest, at home in the arms of God.

Hear him tell you that he is also preparing a place for you where one day you too will be at home with him and your loved ones forever ... allow God's peace to fill your heart and mind now ... rest in the comfort of God's gentle care ...

We take our loved ones by the hand and lead them to you, God of love ... Accept our love and thanksgiving as we give them into your loving care ...

Take our sad and aching hearts and comfort us ...

God of the sorrowing draw near ...

Reflection 2

I invite you now, to take in your hand, the daffodil bulb you received earlier. As you hold it, notice its shape, its texture, its dryness ...

Become aware that this bulb carries within it the possibility of becoming something beautiful ... But in order for this daffodil to appear in the spring, it first needs to be buried in the earth ... For some months it will be hidden in the darkness, out of sight of all of us ... While we may feel or think that nothing is happening during that period of darkness, a wonderful transformation is taking place ...

Then, in early spring you will be surprised to see a healthy, green bud appear above the ground and the bud will go on growing, coming to the fullness of life, until it flowers in all its glory at Easter time ...

I now invite you, to close your eyes ... See in this bulb, a symbol of death and resurrection ... Those whom we loved dearly and who have now gone from us in death leave us feeling that all is finished ...

Imagine yourself, placing this bulb tenderly deep in the dark earth ... Be still ....

Become aware of the darkness ...

You can no longer see the bulb ...

Be aware of the solitude ... allow yourself to experience again the periods of intense darkness and weariness of your days of mourning ...

You find yourself waiting for the pain of loneliness to leave you ...

Be aware of this waiting ... the hope ... the expectation ...

Be ... in the darkness ... listen to the darkness ...

Be aware of the transformation taking place in the bulb beneath the earth ... See tiny green shoots coming from the bulb, pushing their way above the ground ... Notice how you feel ... the darkness lifting ... your hope increasing ... Be aware of that feeling of hope, as the bud continues to grow and to flower into a beautiful yellow blossom, blowing in the spring breeze ...

Be aware of death turning into new life ...

The mists of sadness and loneliness evaporate ... Many buds of new life begin to open ...

Experience, the touch of life ...

The touch of love ...

We invite you then, to take this daffodil bulb home and to plant it in a container of clay ... Leave it for some time in the darkness ... Watch it, nourish it and then bring it into the light ... Wait for the appearance of the green buds in spring.

Let it remind you, of the waiting you are experiencing, as you want the cloud of grieving that covers you to lift ...

As the flower appears in the spring, allow it to remind you that the loved one you grieve for, is now enjoying the fullness of life and love with God in heaven.

At Easter time we will gather in this church to celebrate the resurrection of Jesus, reminding us of our ultimate destiny: we will be asking you to bring your flowering daffodil along to create a spring garden in our church where together we will rejoice that those we've known and loved in this life are at home in the heart of God forever.

The Offertory Procession
During the past year, a number of our parishioners have died as have other relatives and friends elsewhere. In our Offertory procession we will use symbols which remind us yet again of our loved ones whom we remember with love here tonight.
1. ... presents the candle, symbol of our faith and firm hope that our loved ones are with God.
2. ... brings flowers. Flowers are used on many occasions throughout our life, in times of joy and in times of sorrow. Each flower this evening represents the person we have lost and is also a token of our love and thanksgiving to God for the gift they were in our families.
3. ... brings forward the oil, a symbol of healing and strengthening for the journey, which will be used to anoint the bereaved later on in this service.
4. ... and ... carry bread and wine which will be changed into the body and blood of Christ. We too will one day be transformed into new life, for life is changed not taken away.

After Communion each one is anointed for healing and courage.
Songs during the anointing:
The Cloud's Veil[5]
Healing is Your Touch[6]

Closing Prayer:

God, thank you for the special people in our lives whom we are remembering here tonight. We thank you that you are a compassionate God who walks with us in our dark moments of grief and loneliness. We are thankful for all who continue to love and support us through our grief. Continue to be a Light for us, giving us hope, direction and courage. May we now live our lives treasuring the memories of those special people we have known and loved and help us to bring light and hope to others. We make this prayer through Christ Our Lord. Amen.

Concluding words of gratitude, with an invitation to all to remain for a cup of tea and a chat.

Final Song: Enfold Me In Your Love[7]

References

1. Carey Landry & NALR 1993, *I will not forget you,* volume 2
2. Bernadette Farrell, DCP publication 1994
3. Carmel Boyle with reflection by Ger Holton, An Croí, Ashbourne Co Meath
4. Liam Lawton, *In The Quiet,* GIA Publications 2002
5. Text and music by Liam Lawton, arr John McCann, GIA Publications 1998
6. *A Special Collection* by Monica Brown, Emmaus Publications 1997
7. Monica Brown and Emmaus Productions,1997, *One Moment*

A Celebration of the Autumn Years of Life

General Comment
Our senior citizens are a blessing in the community. Their faith, wisdom and commitment need to be valued by all of us.

October, the time of passing from fullness of life into Autumn, 'the season of mists and mellow fruitfulness', is an occasion to highlight and to celebrate the gift of the older members of the community. The ritual takes place in the afternoon when people are more likely to venture out. It's also important to offer transport to and from the venue for those less mobile or housebound.

It's always heartening to hear their responses to such a celebration. They feel affirmed and valued by what takes place.

Introduction
Poets and writers continuously remind us that one hallmark of a truly civilised society is its appreciation and acknowledgement of the importance of the elderly, those special people who have lived life longer than the rest of us, tasted more fully the rhythm of joy and sorrow, loss and gain, disappointment and hope and, when they have reflected on it, are the keepers of a great store of wisdom. That is our reason for being here, to honour those of you now in the autumn years of your life.

Another probable reason – though no one says it too loudly – is because there is a tendency nowadays towards the opposite: a consumer world tends to measure value and worth in terms of work and usefulness, with the suggestion that people too, like products on the shelf, have their use-by and sell-by dates after which they can be discarded.

So today, we gather to celebrate you, to honour the special gift and blessing you are in this community, to pray a blessing on you and to anoint you with the oil of gladness and healing.

Opening song: Gather us O God[1]

Scripture Reading: Luke 2:25-38 Simeon and Anna

Commentary
Simeon and Anna we don't know too much about, but we do know this
much – they were elderly; retired; families reared; had time to be quiet
and reflective, had time for God. Each spent a lot of time in prayer; they
both recognised and pointed to the mystery, recognised the Saviour, the
Promised One.

Song: In The Quiet[2]

Guided Reflection: Symbol: An autumn leaf
Appreciating the many experiences in our lives.
Autumn – a beautiful season. The trees gradually let go of their leaves
and they fall to the ground in an array of colour – of greens, yellows and
browns. There is a mixture of sunshine, wind and rain in this season.
Today you are invited to see in this season, and in the falling of the
leaves, a symbol of the autumn years which you are celebrating at this
time of your life.

I invite you now to hold the leaf in your hand ... notice how it is ...
its shape, its size, how it feels, its colour ... Before you got it today it was
one among many leaves but now it is special, unique to you. Let it symbolise for you all that you are – special, unique, chosen. You hold that
leaf carefully in your hands just as God is holding you carefully in the
palm of his hand. Hear him say to you, today, 'I have chosen you ... I
call you by name.'

The leaf has its wrinkles and blots, reminding you that your life too
has its signs of change, of wear and tear, of maturing! As you look at the
leaf, you notice there the main artery and the various veins going out
from that. Again it symbolises your life, your heart beat, your breath.
Each vein going out from the central one reminds you of the people,
places and experiences you've had that have brought you to this day ...
Recall the people who have been part of your life and give thanks to God
for them today ... Remember too your spouse, maybe the birth of a
child / children, the happy times, the sad times, the successes and the
disappointments in your life, and hand these over to God in a spirit of
gratitude.

Whatever happens in your life, know that God is indeed very close to you ... God has been with you at every stage of your life's journey up to now. In the quietness hear God say your name and he says to you, 'You are precious to me ... I love you.' So, as you continue to hold that leaf in your hand, let it continue to remind you that you are chosen this day. 'I have carved your name on the palm of my hand.' Take a moment now to give thanks to God for all that has been and for all that is in your life now ... Ask a blessing from him as you continue your journey of life. Tell him what you need most in these autumn years ... Hear him tell you not to be afraid: 'I will never forget you.'

Psalm of Contentment
Sacred season of Autumn, be my teacher at this time of my life. You, autumn, are God's gift to me, reminding me of this precious time in my life. From you, I learn the virtue of contentment as I look at your full-coloured beauty in my own life. This is the season of retirement, of full barns and harvested fields.

The cycle of growth has finished and the busy work of giving life is now completed. I sense in you autumn no regrets; you've lived life to the full. Teach me to let go of regrets, hurts and disappointments. Teach me to take stock of what I have given and received in life. May I experience contentment and peace in my life now. May I know too that I am richly blessed because of the abundance of God's gifts to me. Help me, Lord, to take delight in the abundance of the simple things of life which are a true source of joy and contentment this autumn time of my life.

Anointing and Blessing for healing and inner peace
N..., through this anointing may you know how precious you are in God's eyes and in the life of this community. May he bless you with peace and inner strength and may you know his presence at every step of the journey ahead.

Song: Lay Your Hands[3]

Closing Prayer
We thank and praise you, God, for the many blessings in our lives and for bringing us safely to this day. We pray for each other that we may continue to find peace and contentment in our lives. May we always treasure the wisdom of these years and rejoice in sharing our lives with others. Thank you, God, for this time together today.
May God continue to support us all the day long, 'until the shadows lengthen and the evening comes and the busy world is hushed and the fever of life is over and our work is done; then in God's mercy, may God give us a safe lodging and a holy rest and peace at last.'

Blessing of Those in the Autumn Years
'A Blessing For Old Age'[4]

References
1. *A Special Collection* by Monica Brown. Emmaus Productions 1997
2. Liam Lawton, GIA Publications 2002
3. *Abba Father*, Carey Landry, NALR 1977
4. *Anam Chara*, John O Donohue, Bantham Press 1997, page 242

Affirmation and Blessing of those who build up our community

General Comment:
This ritual is devised for those who generally work in a voluntary capacity or for statutory bodies in the greater community of the parish. It is intended for scout leaders, sports leaders, caring groups or agencies in the locality, those working for the elderly, those in family resource centres etc. It is important that the parish recognises and celebrates the important contribution of all those people in building up the community – the Body of Christ in the locality. It is a way of helping these people to see that they are indeed the hands, heart, feet, of Christ today in this place; that in and through them God touches the hearts and lives of others.

Welcome and introduction
We are happy to welcome each of you here to this special celebration. We acknowledge and celebrate the ways in which you contribute to creating a vibrant community in this area. We gather then to thank God for the ways you use your special gifts and to ask God's blessing on you as you continue to play your part in making the community a place of life and love.

Lighting of Candles
I invite you now to come forward and light a candle, naming the group or organisation for which you work. This lighted candle then stands as a symbol of the light you are – the blessing you are in the community.

Reading
One thing stirs me when I look back at my youthful days; it is the fact that so many people gave me something or were something to me without knowing it. Such people had a decisive influence on me; they entered into my life and became powers within me. Much that I should not otherwise have felt clearly or done so effectively was felt or done as it was because I stand, as it were, under the sway of these people. Hence I always think that we all live spiritually by what others have given us in the significant hours of life. If we had before us those who have thus

been a blessing to us and could tell them how it came about, they would be amazed to learn what passed over from their life to ours.
(From *Memories of Childhood and Youth* by Albert Schweitzer)

Quiet time, with reflective music

Scripture Reading: 1 Corinthians 12:12-26, 'One body, many parts'

Song: St Teresa's Prayer[1]

Reflection
The Long View
It helps now and then to step back and take the long view. The Kingdom is not only beyond our efforts; it is even beyond our vision. We accomplish in our lifetime only a tiny fraction of the magnificent enterprise that is God's work. Nothing we do is complete, which is another way of saying that the Kingdom always lies beyond us.
No statement says all that could be said.
No prayer fully expresses our faith.
No confession brings wholeness.
No programme accomplishes fully the mission.
No set of goals and objectives includes everything.
That is what we are about. We plant the seeds that one day will grow. We water seeds already planted knowing that they hold future promise.
We lay foundations that will need further development. We provide yeast that produces effects far beyond our capabilities.
We cannot do everything and there is a sense of liberation in realising that.
This enables us to do something and to do it very well.
It may be incomplete but it is a beginning, a step along the way, an opportunity for the Lord's grace to enter and do the rest.
We may never see the end results but that is the difference between the master builder and the worker.
We are workers, not master builders; ministers, not messiahs.
We are prophets of a future not our own.
Amen.[2]

Guided Meditation:
In the quiet of this evening I invite you to rest and relax for a few moments. Make yourself comfortable and if you wish close your eyes. Be still. Become aware of the sound of the music in the background. You are being invited to reflect quietly on what it is you are doing in this community to make a difference ... Become aware of your gifts ... your energy ... your enthusiasm ... your ability to do what helps others around you. Hear God now speak into the quiet of your heart: 'You are my chosen one ... you are precious to me ... I call you by name ...' How do you react or respond to this special call of God? How does it feel to be chosen and precious in God's eyes?
See now in your mind's eye the people, or the groups with whom you work in the community ... adults, young people or children ... Notice how you relate with these people ... if they were to speak to you now what might they be saying to you? Become aware of the positive contribution you make in each of their lives. Be aware that in doing what you do you are indeed the body of Christ. Hear Jesus tell you that you are his hands, his feet, his voice, his heart going about doing good. Express your thanks to God for the gifts that are yours. Thank him for the people with whom you work and ask him to continue to give you the strength and the generosity to continue sharing your gifts in this way. Slowly become aware again of the music in the background and become aware of the people around you in the room.

Blessing of oil of anointing
Come Spirit of God, bless this oil of anointing. May it be an oil of gladness and strength. We pray that by being anointed and blessed with this oil our hands and hearts will be made strong for the work we do in this community. May each one here continue to be compassionate to human need, strong and gentle in our care and support of one another and always faithful to what we undertake to do. We make this prayer through Christ our Lord. Amen.

Individual Anointing
N... through this holy anointing may you know again how precious you are in God's eyes; and may God's Spirit be upon you.

Song: Here I am Lord[3]

Prayer of Commitment, said together
Lord, we thank you for all the energy for good that is gathered here. We acknowledge that it is not easy to keep going; that moments of disillusionment and doubt are inevitably part of the experience of all who work for a better world. Be with us in our efforts. May we always delight in the good, have love in our hearts and be enablers of those around us. Help us to believe that all that is truly good points beyond ourselves to you who are Goodness itself.
We pray this, through Christ our Lord.
Amen.

References
1. John Michael Talbot 1987, Birdwing Music
2. Oscar Romero
3. Dan Schutte SJ and NALR, 1981

Saint Valentine's Day

General Comment

St Valentines day, 14 February, is a day which is much celebrated in the commercial sense. The advertising campaign starts soon after we've rung in the New Year. I believe it's important for us, as a faith community, to bring the good news message of love, support, care and friendship to bear on this celebration. In the parish context we celebrate it each year under the title: 'Celebrating the Gift of Love and Loving in Our lives.'

We insist that the celebration is all inclusive, that it's not just for couples but for each person, married or single, who acknowledges the need to love and to be loved. We send special invitations to couples who were married in the previous year and to couples due to be married in the coming year. In doing this we think it is important to use the occasion to help them connect with the wider parish group.

Very often in the sharing during the ritual, some participants will tell how they experience love in their homes, in their relationships and in the local community, especially at a time of tragedy or in moments of jubilation. To highlight the fact that this celebration is for everyone, we usually invite individuals and couples to share something of their experience of love and loving in life. This includes, married, single, priests or religious.

Welcome and Introduction
Symbol: Heart of Lights

This celebration is for everyone who believes in friendship, love and affection. It is for everyone who believes in the rich support found in this community. It is a celebration of genuine love among us where God is.

Each of us in our particular areas do what we can to give heart to this place. We all without exception have a place in this. and together with others we make a huge difference.

Tonight as you come forward to light a flame, just be aware of your gift of love and life, and believe that you are a light in the lives of your family, friends and neighbours.

Movement
Each one comes forward to light a flame.

Song: Love Changes Everything[1]

So as we look at all these lights, we see symbols of the light of love,
which shines in us, through us and among us. Tonight then is a time to
celebrate and give thanks for the love within me, which I can share and
for the love that others continue to share with me, with us.
I remember those too from the past who brought light;
I remember those who brought love;
I remember those who brought God into my life.

So Valentine's Day is an occasion in which everyone who loves is included;
yes, for everyone gathered here now, it's 'Appreciation Day' – honouring,
delighting in and appreciating each other.

Words from Scripture
'Where there is love; there is God.'
'As long as we love one another God will live in us.'
'Love never gives up; its faith, hope and patience never fail.'
'A faithful friend is a sturdy shelter; when you find one you have found a
treasure.'

Song: Give Yourself to Love[2]

Guided Meditation
I invite you now … to become quiet … put your feet firmly on the
ground … Relax your shoulders and the muscles of your neck and face
… And leave your hands loosely… on your lap.
    If you wish … close your eyes gently … Take a few really deep breaths
… they can help you to slow down … at the end of the day …
    Go inside yourself … In your mind, find a favourite spot … a quiet
place where you feel at peace … a place which has meant or means a lot
to you … Sit down there … look around … enjoy being there … relax.
    As you sit … you are aware that it is Valentines Day/Eve … For weeks
… the shops have been reminding everyone … cards … hearts… chocolates

... gifts ... You say to yourself, 'But what is it *really* about? ...

You seem to hear a snatch of a song ... *The Power of Love* ... Your mind begins to wander down memory lane.

The power of love! ... the words bring you back to a point in your life when you experienced love ...

Perhaps different occasions come to mind ... try to focus on one ... who was the person ... or the people ... who touched your life with love? When was it? ... what was happening for you? ... Can you recall some of the words ... or the gestures ... which were used ... to convey love ... care ... concern ... comfort ... forgiveness? ... words and gestures ... which made such a difference to you at that time ....

How did *you* feel? ...

Sit with your memories of this time in your life .... Be grateful ...

However, love is not only to be gratefully received, it is there to be given too.

You begin to question yourself ... about how *you* have brought love into the lives of others ...

To whom? ... When? ... Where? ... How? ...

How did it feel for you to be able to share your love with another person or persons ...?

Again be grateful ...

You go back again to Valentine's Day... The Power of Love ... For us Christians, where is God in all this? ...

We are told ... God loves us ... God is Love ... God is Faithful ... He never gives up on us ... He forgives us ...

Sometimes all this happens in a very personal way for us ... between us and him ... But sometimes ... often ... his love comes to us through other people ... and his love reaches other people through us ...

So everyday there are many occasions, little and great, for giving and receiving love ...

Could this too make a difference to my life? ...

It is time to leave that favourite spot ... so look around it before you leave ... come back gently to where you are ... When you are ready ... Slowly and gently ... open your eyes.

Response
What does love, friendship, relationship mean in my life?
Allow time for sharing on this question
Then, a couple, a single person and a religious share their experience of love and loving.

Reflections of the Heart
Saying 'I love you' is so much more than an expression of our feelings.
It is a two-way commitment between hearts, between lives.
It is not expecting too much from each other too soon, but taking time
to build our relationship on trust and respect.
It is recognising our differences as well as our similarities, and seeing
those differences as a way to complement one another.
It is accepting each other's shortcomings, but emphasising the strengths,
encouraging the successes, but still loving during the failures.
It is realising that the things which make each of us special and unique
also make our relationship special and unique.
It is being friends; liking – as well as loving – each other.
It is remembering that, even though we are close, we each deserve distance; that, even though we are together, we each deserve our solitude.
It is sharing the sad and the happy, the wrong and the right;
the worst and the best; and, through everything, still believing
that to say the words 'I love you' is worth it all.

Take a quiet moment to reflect: Who is the person/who are the people
who enrich your life by their love?
Each person writes a name or names on the little paper heart and then moves forward to place it in the centre of the heart of lights. Each one takes a 'Love is' card as they return to their place. (These cards are based on the text of 1 Corinthians 13:4-8.)

Song: If Love had Wings[3]

The Story of the Ring
In a fair and far off land, many centuries ago, a young king was married
to a princess he loved. So, together they lived happily until they learned

one day that duties were to force the king to journey far away. One night before he left, as he walked through the palace grounds, he tossed into a moonlit pond some pebbles he had found. As the lovely ripples widened from where the pebbles fell, the king stood thinking quietly of the wife he loved so well. And remembering on the next day the circles he had seen, he had a golden ring made to fit the finger of the queen. 'There's no ending or beginning to the circles of this band', the king said to his wife, as he slipped it on her hand, 'and that's why I have chosen this golden ring to be a pledge to you, my love will last through all eternity.' And so, since that day, a ring has been the symbol of the beauty of devotion and endlessness of love.

Blessing of Rings
Lord, we ask you to bless these rings. For each of us this endless band speaks of friendship, love and faithfulness. As we continue to wear these rings may they remind us of your never ending care and love of us and help us to continue to be loving in our living and in our giving. We ask this through Christ our Lord, Amen.

Song: Perhaps Love[4]

Renewal of Commitment
Option One
We renew now our commitment to love others whether the other be a life partner, spouse, friend, neighbour, co-worker.
So, we give thanks on this special evening for one another – for the gift of love which we receive and share, for those who help us to know we are treasured and loved for being who we are.
As we celebrate that love now we renew our commitment to love each other in the good times and in the more difficult times of our lives.
We ask that our love for each other will shine as a bright flame to all.
Help us never to take each other for granted but rather to rejoice in the beauty and marvel which the other person is.
May our love always lead to fullness of life with each other and with our God.

Option Two
God of Love
We celebrate and give thanks for the gift of love and loving in our lives.
We commit ourselves this day to each other, to our friends and to all who
share life with us.
We ask your help that we will always be awake to the needs of each other,
needs both spoken and unspoken.
May our love and friendship lead us to fullness of life and to you.
We ask your divine protection from the strong tides of daily difficulties.
Shield us from selfishness and the temptation to be too busy to spend
time with each other.
We thank you for all who have enriched our lives in the past and we pray
that we will be a support to each other and true to each other always.
Amen.

Litany of Thanksgiving
Response: We thank you.
God of love, we thank you today for the many ways we have been given a
touch of your goodness.
For the love that draws us to friendship and fidelity.
For love that leads us to kindness and compassion.
For love that draws us towards the sacred and the serene.
For love that soothes our heartaches and gentles our pain.
For love that sees the worth and beauty in each human being.
For love that reaches out in forgiveness.
For love that offers the hand of warm welcome.
For love that urges us to take risks and have courage.

God, Source of Love, we give you thanks for the way you are present in
all these forms of love. May the many symbols and gestures of this
Valentine's Day remind us of you, O God, holding us all in the
tenderness of your Love.

Song: Enfold Me In Your Love[5]

Final Prayer and Blessing

We thank you, God, the source of all love for this time together. We thank you, God, for the extravagance of your love. We are thankful for the love we have known all through our lives and for the love we continue to experience. Help us always to marvel at the wonder, the beauty and the uniqueness of each person we meet in life.

God, we are grateful for the gift of each one here and for the participation of each one tonight, especially for those who shared their stories, their music and song.

So,
May the beauty of the God of love sing in you.
May the comfort of God wrap around you.
May the goodness of God draw you closer.
May the generosity of God open you to the world.
And may the love of God bring you peace.

'We promise you my God that we shall keep in our heart these friends and every night our heart will go to sleep near their heart. And God said, it is alright.'[6]

References
1. Andrew Lloyd Weber, *Aspects of Love*
2. Kate Wolf, *The Wind Blows Wild*, 1998, Rhino Records
3. Frances Black, *Talk to Me*. Daracd 056, produced by Arty McGlynn and Pearse Dunne
4. Mary O'Hara
5. Monica Brown, CD *Quiet My Soul*, Emmaus Productions 2003
6. Samburu Prayer

Harvest Festival of Thanksgiving

'You, Lord, Have given so much to me.
Give me one more thing – a grateful heart.'

General Comment

Thanksgiving … harvest times … awareness of blessings … gratitude for the gift of life and love … It is indeed good and necessary to help each other to think deeply about all that we have been given. We can be almost overwhelmed by all that is ours. God is so generous to us. In the context of parish life then this celebration in autumn time provides an ideal opportunity to come together to celebrate and give thanks for so much. Traditionally, harvest thanksgiving in Ireland is associated with the fruits of the earth. This ritual, however, goes further to include a celebration of the beauty and wonder of nature all around us and also the acknowledgement of the internal fruits of our lives as individuals and as a community. In inviting people to this gathering they are encouraged to bring along some small item – a picture, a fruit, a vegetable, bread etc – as an offering to signify their gratitude for all they have and are.

The preparation and general décor of the room for the celebration is very important. Baskets of fruit, vegetables, bread, flowers, wall hangings, banners and lights are placed around the room so as to focus participants on the theme.

Welcome and Introduction

Our autumn Service of Thanksgiving draws us together again. This is the 'season of mists and mellow fruitfulness'.

The harvest is almost complete. Across the land fruits, vegetables and grains have been harvested, gardens and fields give of their gifts.

Sometimes, it is only when produce is gathered and the grain is harvested that the fruits of the earth are seen in all their bounty.

We too are asked to count our blessings even when the reaping at first looks sparse and lean.

This season, long regarded as special, is celebrated in so many places with festivals of thanksgiving.

Nancy Wood: 'I must be thankful for what is and stop thinking about what is not.' There are so many gifts to be unwrapped every day if we are awake to their presence and willing to accept them. The late Eddie Fitzgerald, in an article written shortly before his death entitled, 'Letting Illness Make the Best of Me', talked of his thanksgiving diary where each night he wrote down five things for which he was thankful in that day.

So tonight we celebrate life, each other, the beauty of creation, the fruits of the earth and all who work to provide for our needs.

We are thankful for what nourishes us, not just physically but mentally, spiritually and emotionally also.

The magic word: 'Thank You' is all important.

I invite you now to relax and to allow the basic elements of God's creation to ring around us, gracing us with their wisdom and encircling us.

Fire: We celebrate the gift of fire.
Fire has held mystery since the beginning of time.
Let there be light!
God spoke light into the void, a light that brightens our lives.
The light is in our hands against the darkness.
May the power, the warmth, the passion and mystery of fire be given us.

Earth: God gifts us with the earth. Tonight we claim this gift.
The earth nourishes us as a mother. It is by the fruits of this earth we live. We dig and grow and know its power.
We pray that we might walk gently on this earth.

Air: God gives us the gift of air, air that is invisible yet around and within us. We breathe this air every moment of our existence. Without it we die. We reverence the air which sustains all of life.

Water: We praise our God who gifts us with water. It is so necessary, precious and pure. We claim the water of life whose rush announces the birth of a baby; the water of life which nourishes seeds and plant roots deep in the earth. We celebrate water, water of our life.

Song: Celebrate and Dance with Joy[1]

A Psalm Reflection
Lord, your greatness is seen in all the world!
Your praise reaches up to the heavens.
It is sung by all Creation.
When I look at the sky, which you have made,
at the moon and the stars which you have set in their places,
what are we that you God should think of us?
What are we that you should care for us?
O sun and moon, bless the Lord,
All you works of the Lord, praise him.
O fire and heat, bless the Lord,
winter and summer, praise him forever.
Ice and snow, bless the Lord,
light and darkness praise him.
Birds of the air bless the Lord,
praise and exalt God forever.

Guided Reflection
Be quiet and still ... Be aware of how you are in yourself at this time
tonight ... Allow your body to relax ... Be aware of the sounds around
you ... Let them slowly fade into the distance ... Hear your God inviting
you tonight to be still ... With hands open on your lap hold the symbol
you brought with you ...
I invite you now to harvest, to gather in the many gifts that are yours, to
notice what has been placed in the storehouse of your heart ...
Take these moments to remember, to reflect on what it is you are really
grateful for in your life ... What are the treasures you want to gather into
your thanksgiving basket tonight?
Maybe there are some big things that stand out, that are obvious ... Be
grateful for them ... Perhaps too there are the small, bite-sized pieces of
your life ... being able to get out of bed in the morning ... the cup of
coffee/tea ... having enough to eat ... clothes to wear ... Whatever it is
... take a moment now to be thankful. These little blessings (big bless-

ings) are often presumed ... taken for granted in our busy lives.

Recall times you enjoyed the beauty of nature all around ... a walk in the park; the wind blowing, the variety of flowers ... a sunrise or sunset ... the sky at night ... moon and stars ... the mountains and hills ... allow some of these into your awareness and give thanks to God, the Creator of it all.

Take time to savour the gift of water ... the flowing rivers ... being refreshed by drinking the cold water or plunging into a pool ...

Be thankful ...

Hear in your imagination now the many sounds of nature – birdsong, wind, rain, buzzing of bees ... and give God thanks ...

Recall the many people in your life ... who are they? ... See their faces in your imagination now ... the people who are part of your life each day ... friends, family, work colleagues, public servants ... see them, name their names to yourself ... In what ways are they a blessing in your life? ... Be grateful for each one of them now ...

What about the internal fruits in your life? ... the many experiences of the past year? Have you taken time to reflect on them? ... Perhaps you have experienced much and harvested little?

What are the fruits in your life? ... What do you want to savour of what you experienced this past year? ... Perhaps too you could look at your struggles, your frustrations and irritations and discover the hidden blessings maybe in them ... Perhaps it is only when someone or something is absent or lost that we really appreciate them ...

So gather into the inner room of your life the harvest of your life, so precious ... Stand before these blessings and take a long, grateful look ... Be aware that God exists in and through all these gifts of creation ... all of which nourishes your life.

Count your blessings ... God is lavish in love, generous in the outpouring of goodness ... Cherish deeply all that you are and have ...

'Praise the Lord, my soul;

I will praise and thank God as long as I live.

I will sing to God all my life.'

Stretch your arms high and wide above your head saying: I thank you God for the gift of this day, this moment.

Hold your arms out turn to right and left saying: I thank you God for each person around me in life.

Hold your arms towards the Sacred Space saying: I thank you God for all the fruits of the earth which nourish us every day.

Stretch arms out, slightly apart with palms up, saying: I open myself to receive the gifts that you God are offering me each day.

Stretch your arms out and palms down, saying: I wish to be generous, God, in sharing the gifts of my life with others.

Cross hands over your heart and bow gently, saying: May I always be aware, God, of how blessed I am.

Movement:
Each person moves forward and places in the sacred space the item of food which they brought.

Litany
Let us give thanks to God our Father for all the gifts that are freely given to us.

For the beauty and wonder of God's creation, in earth and sky and sea.
We thank you Lord.

For all that is gracious in men and women, revealing the image of Christ.
We thank you Lord.

For our daily food and drink, our homes and families, and our friends.
We thank you Lord.

For health and strength to work, and leisure to rest and play.
We thank you Lord.

For all these, for every breath of life we breathe, for our very heartbeat, and for our every footstep on this good earth.
We thank you Lord.

Let us pray.
We thank you, God, for you are indeed our Father and Creator. You have given us life and you know us all by name. You hold the world in your hands. We thank you for giving us freedom and life; the air we breathe; the sun that shines; the rain that gives growth; the soil and the seeds; the grass and corn; the vegetables and fruits; the animals and fish; our milk

and butter; and for all these things we give you thanks.
Come, giver of all good gifts, and bless us. Let us thank our God today
and always.

A Circle Dance
is done by some of the participants by which they reverence the fruits of the
earth and of our lives, and share them with others.

A Thanksgiving Blessing
May an abundance of gratitude burst forth from you as you reflect upon
what you have received.
May thanksgiving overflow in your heart and often be proclaimed in
your prayer.
May your basket of blessings surprise you with its variety of gifts.
May you always be open and ready to share your blessings with others.
May you never take any day, any moment for granted.
May 'Thanks be to God' be the prayer of your heart each night and
May you never forget God who loves you and lavishes you with so much.

Final Song: Sing and Dance[2]

References
1. Words and music by Monica Browne and Emmaus productions 1997
2. Monica Brown on CD *Praise and Blessings*, Emmaus Productions 1999

Sundown Service

(Giving thanks for the year ending and welcoming the New Year)

Symbols: 2 Parish Calendars *(One of year ending and one of the new year)*
Carol: 'O Come All Ye Faithful' or some other appropriate song

Gathering Words

We gather as the sun begins to set on the year 20--. We reflect together on the year that is coming to an end, looking back with gratitude, maybe with a sense of relief, and then looking forward, with expectation and courage.

Lighting of Candles on the Wreath

As we bring light to these candles we bring light to the heart of this time of prayer.
Time moves on, it waits for no person. Each moment in time is pure gift and there is in God's plan a time for everything. All time is God's time. We let go of the past and welcome what is to come.

Scripture Reading: Ecclesiastes 3:1-8 For everything there is a Season …

Reflection

My life is a gift given, not in years, but a day at a time.
Today is the day the Lord has made for me, and he planned it to be the most important day of my life.
Yesterday is gone, never to return. I must not worry about it but leave it in the hands of God.
Tomorrow and all it holds is God's secret and its coming is not assured. Only today is mine.
Each day, arranged by God with infinite wisdom and goodness is his gift, his act of love for me.
In thanksgiving, I will offer him every day the gift of myself, my prayers, works, joys and sufferings.
Dear Lord, receive it graciously.

Guided Reflection

Rest in the quiet of the evening ... The last sunset of the year 20-- is beginning to set. Be aware that God is dwelling in love within you and around you ...

Place your hands on your lap, palms up and open.

In your mind, place in your hands the people and events of the past Year – your loved ones ... your neighbours and people of the parish with whom you interact ... those with whom you have had differences and struggles ... the people, events and situations that have been significant for you during the year ... anyone or anything else that comes to your mind or heart ...

Offer each of these people and situations to God in a spirit of thanksgiving.

Now mentally place in your open hands all of your gifts of the past year: your happiness ... your successes ... your insights and awareness ... those who were an inspiration to you ... the difficulties from which you emerged a stronger person ... anything else that seems like a gift to you in the past year ... offer your prayer of thanks for all these gifts, for the year just ending, with all its blessings and pains ...

As you hold your palms open on your lap, mentally offer those open hands to God, a sign of your openness and trust in God, and accept whatever this New Year brings for you ...

Place in those open hands your whole life, all your concerns, cares, hopes, dreams, joys ...

Place there too any specific people with whom you are specially bonded or hope to be in the New Year ...

Offer your very life to God now and pray your prayer of hope as you prepare to begin a New Year.

God is saying to you now, 'Do not remember the former things; I am about to do a new thing' (Isaiah 43:16-19)

I invite you now to stand ... raise your hands (palms up)

Once again, place all of your past and your future in those hands and give all in trust to God who always accompanies you on the journey of life ...

For what has been, we say *thanks*.

For what will be, we say *yes*.

Watching the Sun go down
All process to the window to watch the sun go down.
Don't let the sun go down on your anger …
Let go of the past …
Forgive yourself and others …
Be thankful …

Sing: Alleluia

Lighting of 12 candles, one for each month of the year
In January, the month of darkness and frost – Be with us Lord.
In February, the month of rain, wind, and snow – Be with us Lord.
In March, the month of farmers, lambs and new life – Be with us Lord.
In April, the month of swallows, growth and green grass – Be with us Lord.
In May, the month of the cuckoo, flowers and summer – Be with us Lord.
In June, the month of examinations, the mid-summer sun – Be with us Lord.
In July, the month of holidays, the dry grass, and the summer's end – Be with us Lord.
In August, the month of harvest, wheat and corn – Be with us Lord.
In September, the month of fruits, schools and St Michael – Be with us Lord.
In October, the month of falling leaves, nuts and Halloween – Be with us Lord.
In November, the month of the dead, the souls and the saints – Be with us Lord.
In December, the month of the gift, the light and our Saviour – Be with us Lord. (Ref: *Jubilee Resource Book 10*)

Procession around church with lit candles while the song, The Deer's Cry[1] *is played.*

Reflection

So, as we let go of the past, we walk confidently into the New Year. We do not know what or who will surprise us along the way. We can only see life for the present moment. But we can risk the road because we have the tremendous assurance that God goes with us as Our Light, Our Hope, Our Strength.

We trust that there will be enough strength and beauty amid all the pain to sustain us and to urge us forward.

God is offering each of us a new beginning with the beginning of the New Year. Let's accept it with gratitude and faith in our hearts as we travel as pilgrims on the Road of Life.....

Prayers of Intercession

Response: Generous God, fill our hearts.

The God of life is always with us, breathing energy and compassion into our hearts. We thank him for the year just ending and we open ourselves to whatever he is offering us in the year 20--. We pray.

We pray for the gift of gratitude that we may be always thankful for the gift of each new day. We pray.

We pray for the gift of hope that we may be able to meet the challenges of each day with courage. We pray.

We pray for the gift of joy that we may always delight in the beauty and goodness of each human being and in the mystery of your love in them. We pray.

We pray for the gift of peace that we may be in harmony with each other, accepting differences as a gift. We pray.

Anyone who wishes to make their own prayer. We pray.

A New Year's Blessing

May you awake each morning with thank you on your lips and in your heart, recognising that all is a gift, that all is a blessing.

May your friendship with God be strong and healthy. May that love be both a comfort and a challenge as you struggle to find your way in the New Year.

May your life this New Year be a living legacy to your God.

An Irish Blessing
May the road rise to meet you.
May the wind be always at your back.
May the sun shine warm upon your face,
and may the rain fall softly on your fields.
Until we meet again, may **God hold** you in the palm of his hand.

Closing Prayer
Lord, you are in this place this evening as we give thanks for the past year and as we welcome the new. We are walking into mystery. Fill us with your strength, cover us with your peace, help us to know that we are in your hands, we are under your protection, we are covered by your love.

We face the future, not knowing what the days and months will bring for us. We ask you now to walk with us into the coming year, to guide us on our way and to keep us from all harm.

Lord, give us the eyes to see you in everyone and every place, ears to hear your call in the people and situations around us, hands to do your work and hearts to respond to your love. Amen.

Final Song: Journey Blessing[2]

References
1. *The Pilgrim,* Shaun Davey, Tara Music Company 1998
2. On CD *We Will Remember,* Carmel Boyle and Ger Holton 2002

From the rising of the sun to its setting we remember them

A Service of Remembrance for those who have miscarried, had a still birth or lost a baby through any circumstance

General Comment

This service is very important in every parish. We have discovered that people of all ages come along as they need the opportunity to acknowledge their grief for a baby who has died in the past. There are many people who have not had an opportunity to name, to pray for and indeed to give expression to their feelings of sadness at the loss of their little ones.

This is a service which needs to be planned and carried out with great sensitivity.

The Miscarriage Association of Ireland and the Irish Stillbirth Association are most willing to have some of their members present at such a service. They bring the special book of Remembrance along and families are invited (if they haven't already done so) to enter the name or names of their babies who have died. For many this is a very important moment. Up until then some would not have given a name to the baby. It's also helpful to have members of the above associations there to mingle with people over the cup of tea because contact is made which can continue to be a great support to families into the future. As people enter they receive a candle and a star on which nis written: 'I have carved your name on the palm of my hand.'.

Gathering Song: Where Healing Can Begin[1]

Welcome and Introduction

The death of a baby, whether at birth, soon afterwards or in the weeks and months before the due date is traumatic.

Each one of you here has come because at some time in the past or more recently, you lost a baby or perhaps many babies through one circumstance or another and you carry deep within you the pain of that loss. The death of a baby is the most tragic of losses because you grieve not only for the tiny baby that died before birth or soon after, but for who that baby would become. There is sadness and disappointment that the hopes and dreams you had for them would never be realised. So, you grieve, not only for what was, but for what might have been. You probably have struggled or are still struggling with the questions arising in your hearts – 'why me?', 'why us?', 'why is life so unfair?', 'what did we do wrong?' These are the questions for which there are usually no answers but they are our way of trying to make sense of what happened and to find meaning. This is a normal part of grieving.

For some here the loss of your baby may have been a long time ago and perhaps some people expect you to have put that experience behind you, and you can feel so alone in your feelings of grief and loss. For others, there may be the feeling of incompleteness. There never was a real recognition that the baby you lost was a human being and you struggle with that lack of recognition.

It becomes more and more difficult perhaps to let go because you may never have had the opportunity to see or to speak about that baby. So we hope this service provides you with that opportunity to acknowledge that child or these children.

We gather then as a Christian Community in solidarity with each other to acknowledge the pain, the sorrow, the loss. We also look beyond the pain and suffering to treasure the child who continues to travel the journey of life with us in a different way and who will always live in our memories and in the story of our family.

We also remember tonight all those who cannot be here and those who have no prayer to offer because their grief has overcome their faith. We hope and pray that one day their faith will be renewed.

Opening Prayer
Let us pray: Eternal God Source of all life, we remember our babies with love and we give thanks. We bring our memories, our hopes, our dreams and our disappointments. Open our eyes to see, our ears to hear and our hearts to know your healing love.
We make this prayer through Christ our Lord. Amen.

Scripture Reading: Matthew 19:13-15, 'Let the children come to me ...'

Lighting of candles as each one remembers their little ones

Placing of these in the sacred space

See in this flame, the light of life in our saddened lives.

God our Father, source of all light, you revealed Christ to us as the Light of the world. May these candles dispel the darkness in our hearts and illuminate us with the brightness of the Holy Spirit. May these tiny lights be a reminder to us that the light of your presence lives in us all, even from the first moments of our existence.

We now go and place these candles in our sacred space where they will continue to burn brightly throughout our service.

Song: Wonder Child[2]

Guided Meditation/Reflection followed by the laying of stars with lights.
I invite you now to hold in you hand the star you received on the way in. On it are printed God's reassuring words about the place of your baby in his plan, 'I have carved your name on the palm of my hand.'

If you haven't already done so, perhaps you'd like to write a name – the name of the baby if you had a name for him/her whom you are remembering here ... *Music played*

We play music and ask you just to relax ... If you wish, close your eyes or just focus on something in front of you ...

This is something you may find easy to do or it may be difficult. Either way, just stay with it and if you find it hard to concentrate just listen to the music.

Become aware of the sounds around you and then allow those sounds to slowly fade into the background of your awareness.

Become aware of how you are feeling as you sit here. Take a deep breath, release it and relax.

You are here to remember and to give thanks for the baby or babies you carried in the womb and who are no longer with you.

Quietly call to mind the hopes the dreams you had for your baby as you were aware of your pregnancy. Maybe it was a time of anxiety and fear or perhaps there was much joy and excitement as you looked forward to the baby. Had you told others yet of your pregnancy?

And now, allow yourself to recall, to remember the time you lost the baby ... Can you remember the circumstances, how it happened? Who was with you? How did you feel? About yourself? About people? And what about God? Did you have any sense of God being near you at the time or did you feel God was far away? Maybe you were angry with God, with life, with people. Whatever the feelings were then just allow yourself to get in touch with them now. Know that your feelings are OK. They are normal and necessary. Did you ever have the opportunity to talk with another person about your feelings? Were you able to tell God how you felt? Perhaps now you can move on and remember the time since you lost your child, how that has been for you.

From where you are now just imagine yourself looking back at how you were then. Look back on that time ... how do you feel now as you look at yourself then? Is there anything you'd like to say to yourself or to your child or anyone else? Imagine God is there; what does he say? Is there anything you'd like to say to God now?

Now you have the chance to allow God into that space in your life. Can you listen to what he has to say to you?

'I will never forget you; I have carved your name on the palm of my hand. Don't be afraid, I am with you' ...

This service is an invitation to you to try to let go of the pain, the hurt, the regrets or whatever you're carrying and to let God be there, offering healing, new life, hope and encouragement.

God draws near to help you. Tell him how you feel; he's big enough to take your anger and your pain-filled words and he promises to be with you.

We know that children, including babies in the womb, have a special place in God's heart ... Jesus says, 'See that you do not despise any of these little ones. Their angels in heaven are always in the presence of my Father in heaven ... Our Father in heaven does not want any of these little ones to be lost.'

Be reassured that your baby/babies are safe in Jesus' arms ... So, quietly and gently become aware again of the sounds around; of the seat supporting your body and become aware again of the people around you in this place.

Blessing of the stars
Lord God, such is your care for all you have made that you mark the fall of even the tiny sparrow. Bless these stars that bear the names of beloved babies who died and are now born again in you. May these stars become a treasured memory and a reminder of their brief lives.

Reflection:
I took my burden to the Lord to cast and leave it there,
I knelt and told him of my plight and wrestled deep in prayer.
But rising up to go on my way I felt a deep despair,
For as I tried to trudge along my burden was still there.
Why didn't you take my burden Lord?
Oh won't you take it please?
Again I asked the Lord for help,
His answering words were these:
'My child, I want to help you out; I long to take your load.
I want to bear your burden too as you walk along life's road.
But this you must remember – This one thing you must know – I cannot take your burden – until you let it go.'[3]

Blessings of Oils and Anointing for inner peace and healing
N… through this holy anointing may you know again how precious you are in God's eyes; and may God's Spirit be upon you to heal your brokenness and to bring light to your darkness.

Song: Lay your hands[4] *while anointing is going on*

A sharing of one woman's personal experience of loss

Prayers of Intercession
Prayer for Mothers
We pray that all mothers who have suffered the great pain of losing the child of their womb may experience the loving protection of Mary the Mother of God. Through her intercession we ask that these mothers be comforted in their sadness and loss, that they be filled with joy and hope and know your peace.
Lord hear us.

Prayer for Fathers
God, our Father, you know the pain experienced by fathers. We ask you now to stay with these fathers, grant them the acceptance and hope that only you can give and fill them with the fullness of your Spirit.
Lord hear us.

Prayer for Families
Let us remember in a special way the brothers, sisters, uncles, aunts and grandparents of the babies who are being remembered here. Lord, help us to know that your love is great at our times of loss.
Lord hear us.

Prayer for those who suffer this loss alone
Lord, we pray for all those who suffered in the past and who now suffer in isolation the loneliness and anguish of loss of life within the womb, whatever the circumstances of that loss. Enfold all who suffer in this way in your healing peace.
Lord hear us.

Prayer of Thanksgiving
O Lord, we thank you for all the people here as we all come together to remember with love those short lives that have touched us all so deeply.
Lord hear us.

Reflection: Rock Them Gently
Rock them gently, Lord, our daughters and sons
Rock them gently till our time comes
Stroke them softly, with all our love
Bring them our prayers on the wings of a dove
Sing to them quietly and ease all our fears
Rock them gently, Lord, our precious little dears.

A Litany of Remembrance
In the rising of the sun and its going down, We remember them.
In the blowing of the wind and in the chill of winter, We remember them.

In the blueness of the sky and in the warmth of summer, We remember them.
In the rustling of leaves and the beauty of autumn, We remember them.
In the beginning of the year and when it ends, We remember them.
When we are lost and sick at heart, We remember them.
When we have joys we yearn to share, We remember them.
So long as we live, they too shall live, for they are part of us, and we remember them.

Song: Fleetingly Known[5]

Fleetingly known yet ever remembered
These are our children now and always.
These whom we see not, we will forget not,
Morning and evening all of our days.

Lives that touched our lives, tenderly, briefly,
Now in the one light, living always.
Names in our hearts now, safe from all harm now,
We will remember, all of our days.

As we recall them, silently name them.
Open our hearts Lord, now and always.
Grant to us grieving, love for the living,
Strength for each other all of our days.

Safe in your peace Lord, hold these your children.
Grace, light and laughter, grant them each day;
Cherish and hold them, till we may know them
When to your glory we find a way.

Closing Prayer
Lord Jesus Christ, who took little ones into your arms and blessed them,
we release our babies into your care.
We give you our aching hearts and the questions no one can answer.
We look to you for comfort.
Help us to keep trusting even in the darkness and let hope be born again
in our hearts.
Amen.

References
1. Carey Landry and NALR 1993, *I Will Not Forget You,* Vol. 2
2. Mary Black, Darac 075
3. Helen Steiner Rice
4. Carey Landry
5. Words: Anonymous, Tune: *Morning has Broken, Bunessan*

Reconciliation Service in Preparation for Easter

Introduction

Welcome to the Service of Reconciliation. We have journeyed together through Lent and are gathered to hear and respond to the call of renewal and conversion which is at the heart of Lent. We come with our thirst for forgiveness and inner healing. We gather around the cross which is the central symbol of Holy Week, a symbol of the dark forces in human nature which put Jesus to death, but also a sign of hope, a sign of the enduring love of God for each of us.

Jesus' whole mission was to reconcile us to God. The religious leadership of the time was shocked and appalled at how ready he was to forgive, to restore, to heal and bind up wounds. 'When I am lifted up,' he said, 'I will draw all people to myself' and so he does.

Tonight, we will allow the cross of Jesus to speak to us of our need for forgiveness and of God's desire to touch us with peace.

Opening Prayer

Gracious God, we thank you for the gift of life; we thank you for creating us in your own image and likeness even though, through hardness of heart and our sinfulness we sometimes distort and frustrate your design for us.

Gathered as your family, we ask you now to open our hearts again to your Word and make us responsive to it in a spirit of generosity and courage.

Scripture Reading: Ezechiel 11:17-20

Guided Reflection and Examination of Conscience
(Using a stone as a symbol)

I invite you now to enter into the quiet and peace of this sacred place. You have come away from the busyness of life just to be, to let God find a home in your heart, to allow yourself to reflect on the areas of your life in need of God's forgiveness and healing.

Allow yourself to relax … Let go of what may have preoccupied you this day or during the past week and enter into the now …

Notice the sounds around you … Then, allow them fade into the background … Be aware of your breathing … Relax … Hold in your hand the stone you received on the way in … Feel it … its shape … its firmness … This symbolises the areas of your life that are not in harmony with God's plan for you. It represents the burden of wrongdoing, which you may be carrying and for which you wish to ask forgiveness.

I ask you now in your imagination to be in the scene of the gospel story that was just read to us. Jesus is there on the steps of the temple … Where are you? … Are you among the crowd condemning this person? … Are you closer to the person being condemned? … Or maybe you are on neutral ground …

Jesus bends down and writes in the dirt … the crowd is mumbling … Jesus acts as though he does not hear them … But soon no one is speaking … you sense what they are all thinking. You watch as one man drops his stone and turns and walks away. He knows he is a sinner … Next, a young woman departs, the stone falling from her fingers; she knows that she could be a better person too …

The faces of two young people are sad as they turn and leave together, stones dropping to the dirt.

As you watch them you can only guess that they have all taken this time to look into their hearts and discover their own personal truth … that they are each a sinner … You continue to watch people leaving … they are now empty handed … the ground is littered with deadly stones.

Jesus moves now from this person whom he has forgiven and he is moving towards you … you sense that Jesus knew you were there all along. He walks over to you and looks at you with the same care and attention he gave to this person who was condemned. Jesus invites you to sit on the temple steps with him … and as you sit together, hear him ask you to share what weighs you down; why your heart is so heavy … why your heart hurts.

Hear Jesus tell you that he knows and understands that it is painful. Allow yourself at this time to be open and to share with Jesus all that is in your heart … about yourself … about your relationships … about anything that bothers you.

Feel Jesus lean in closer toward you to hear all that you are saying.
Hear Jesus respond to what you have shared. See the deep caring in his
eyes … feel his mercy, love and forgiveness.
Listen now as Jesus prays for your hurt to be healed and for your heart to
be filled with peace. Hear Jesus thank you for the gift of who you are.
Hear him tell you to have courage … Feel the warmth and gentle weight
as Jesus places his hands on your head. Listen as he prays for your heal-
ing. Notice how you are feeling now … you wonder if it is what the con-
demned sinner must have felt.
Jesus is telling you that he is inviting you to a fuller and happier life.
He asks you to be a true friend of his … Hear Jesus promise you that he
will always be there to help you.
As Jesus looks at you, feel his promise to be with you always in your
hurts and your joys and in your struggles to succeed.
You must leave Jesus now to take up the challenge to live life more fully.
You are confident that he is with you.
Be aware of your breathing … of the seat beneath you … the floor under
your feet … people around you … Open your eyes.
I invite you now to go to one of the confessors to make your individual
confession. Take the stone with you and after confessing go and drop it
in the container in the sacred space before returning to your place.

Song: Christ Be Our Light[1]

*A number of people take a light to the confessional points. While people go to
the confessors, appropriate songs can be sung or soft music played over the
sound system so as to maintain an atmosphere of quiet reflection.*
*When all have been to confession, the candles are brought back and placed
around the cross at the centre of the gathering.*

Closing Prayer

Confessors extend their hands in a final blessing

Closing Song

Reference
1. Bernadette Farrell, DCP Publications, 1994

Reconciliation Service during Holy Week

Note

This Service takes place after the community has travelled around the estates of the parish and taken part in the Stations of the Cross. Our Celebration of the Passion then incorporates the Sacrament of Reconciliation. We have found that this is an ideal time and way to celebrate Good Friday.

Introduction

We have followed the Way of the Cross around the parish and have reflected on how the passion impacts on our own journey in life. We each carry the cross of pain and suffering and we draw strength from uniting our sufferings with those of Christ. What a rich opportunity we are now given to experience the healing mercy of God in the Sacrament of Reconciliation. As the body of Christ here, we enter into a time of prayer, reflection, repentance and celebration. Our sin affects not only ourselves but the community of the family and parish here. When we sin, this community is less whole. No matter how fine the threads of our community are, when they are woven together, we are strong and whole.

Gathering Song: Stay Here *or* Jesus, Remember Me[1]

Greeting

Leader: Our community is like a fragile fabric, woven together from many threads.
All: When the threads are weak, our community is weak.
Leader: Our community is like fragile fabric, with some broken threads.
All: When the threads are broken, our community is broken.
Leader: Our community is like fragile fabric, with some colourful threads and some strong threads.
All: When the threads are strong, our community is forgiven and healed.
Leader: Let us pray:
Loving God, you are the weaver who binds us together. You are the healer

who mends our brokenness. You are the one who forgives us no matter how many times we come to you.
We want to leave behind us all the things that spoil the cloth of our families and our parish community.

First Reading
We must work to use our talents and energies, develop our strengths, avoid those things that are obstacles to the full and healthy life that we seek. We are called to co-operate in the daily stuff of living. In the ordinariness of life we give generously, we deal with the obstacles and the frustrations patiently and gently, we face ourselves and each other honestly and with compassion. We are called to live life with a big heart.
During the following, as the reading is being done, someone will come and weave a thread in the incomplete weaving which will be in front of the altar.

Leader: Trust is a ribbon that ties us to one another.
We weave the thread of trust through the cloth of our community.
Weave the first strip

Song: Healing is your Touch[2]

Leader: A thread of courage ties the weak to the strong, ties the sick to the healthy.
We weave the thread of courage through the cloth of our community
Weave the second strip

Song: Healing is Your Touch

Leader: There is a ribbon of commitment and daily giving that binds our community together.
We weave the thread of commitment through the cloth of our community.
Weave the third strip

Song: Healing is Your Touch
Leader: The power of Jesus threads through us and empowers us all.
We weave the thread of power through the cloth of our community.
Weave the fourth strip

Song: Healing is Your Touch

Leader: Hope is a thread that leads us towards the vision of the kingdom. We weave the thread of hope through the cloth of our community.
Weave the fifth strip

Song: Healing is Your Touch

Scripture: John :18:1-9
When He had said this, Jesus went with his disciples across the Kedron Valley to where there was a garden, into which he and his disciples entered. Judas his betrayer also knew the place, because Jesus had often met there with his disciples. So Judas got a band of soldiers and guards from the chief priests and the Pharisees and went there with lanterns, torches, and weapons. Jesus, knowing everything that was going to happen to him, went out and said to them 'Whom are you looking for?' They answered him, 'Jesus, the Nazarene.' He said to them, 'I am he.' Judas his betrayer was also with them. When he said to them, 'I am He,' they turned away and fell to the ground. So he again asked them, 'Whom are you looking for?' They said, 'Jesus the Nazarene.' Jesus answered, 'I told you that I am he. So if you are looking for me, let these men go.' This was to fulfil what he had said. 'I have not lost any of those you gave me.'

Leader: Like Judas, we accept positions of trust in our families and our community. Sometimes we abuse that trust, betraying the visions and actions of others, as we pretend to support them, even with a kiss.
The thread is cut

Leader: The thread is broken. And so we pray:
All: Forgive us, O God, when we break the thread of trust.

Scripture. Mark: 14:48-52
Jesus said to them in reply, 'Have you come out as against a robber, with swords and clubs, to seize me? Day after day I was with you, teaching in the temple area, yet you did not arrest me; but that the Scriptures may be fulfilled.' And they all left him and fled. Now a young man followed him wearing nothing but a linen cloth about his body. They seized him, but he left the cloth behind and ran off naked.

Leader: Like the disciples, we have courage when we have the support of others but we often step back in fear when the responsibility falls to us.
The thread is cut

Leader: The thread is broken. And so we pray:
All: Forgive us, O God, when we break the thread of courage.

Scripture: John 18:15-18, 25-27
Simon Peter and another disciple followed Jesus. Now the disciple was known to the high priest and he entered the courtyard of the high priest with Jesus. But Peter stood at the gate outside. So the other disciple, the acquaintance of the high priest, went out and spoke to the gatekeeper and brought Peter in. Then the maid who was the gatekeeper said to Peter, 'You are not one of this man's disciples, are you?' He said, 'I am not.' Now the slaves and the guards were standing around the charcoal fire that they had made, because it was cold and were warming themselves. Peter was also standing there keeping warm. They said to him, 'You are not one of his disciples?' He denied it and said, 'I am not.' One of the slaves of the high priest, a relative of the one whose ear Peter had cut off, said, 'Didn't I see you in the garden with him?' Again Peter denied it. And immediately the cock crowed.

Leader: Like Peter, we are often passionate in what we say about our commitment to you, Jesus, but we lack the courage of our convictions when we are faced with the challenge.
The thread is cut

Leader: The thread is broken. And so we pray:
All: Forgive us, O God, when we break the thread of commitment.

Scripture: John 18:12-14, 19-24
So the band of soldiers, the tribune and the Jewish guards seized Jesus, bound him, and brought him to Annas first. He was the father-in-law of Caiaphas who was high priest that year. It was Caiaphas who had counselled the Jews that it was better that one man should die rather than the people. The high priest questioned Jesus about his disciples and about his doctrine. Jesus answered him, 'I have spoken publicly to the world. I have always taught in the synagogue or in the temple area where all the

Jews gather, and in secret I have said nothing. Why ask me? Ask those who heard me, what I said to them. They know what I said.' When he had said this, one of the temple guards standing there, struck Jesus and said 'Is this the way you answer the high priest?' Jesus answered him, 'If I have spoken wrongly, testify to the wrong; but if I have spoken rightly, why do you strike me?' Then Annas sent him bound to Caiaphas, the high priest.

Leader: We pray that your kingdom will come, but often, like the Jewish authorities, when we see Jesus empowering others, we fear the loss of our own power.
The thread is cut

Leader: The thread is broken. And so we pray:
All: Forgive us, O God, when we break the thread of your empowerment in our community.

Scripture: John 19:5-7, 13-16
Once more Pilate went out and said to them, 'Look I am bringing him out to you, so that you may know that I find no guilt in him.' So Jesus came out wearing the crown of thorns and the purple cloak. And he said to them, 'Behold the man!' When the chief priests and the guards saw him, they cried out, 'Crucify him, crucify him!' Pilate said to them, 'Take him yourselves and crucify him: I find no guilt in him.' ... Pilate tried to release him but the Jews cried out, 'If you release him, you are not a friend of Caesar. Everyone who makes himself a king, opposes Caesar.' When Pilate heard these words, he brought Jesus out and seated him on the judge's bench, in the place called stone-pavement, in Hebrew, Gabbatha. It was the preparation day for the Passover and it was about noon. He said to the Jews, 'Behold your King.' They cried out, 'Take him away, take him away! Crucify him!' Pilate said to them, 'Shall I crucify your king?' The chief priests answered, 'We have no king but Caesar.' Then he handed him over to them to be crucified.

Leader: Like the crowds, we are carried along by waves of hope; but when the tide turns, we give up on our vision and lose hope.
The thread is cut

Leader: The thread is broken. And so we pray:
All: Forgive us, O God, when we break the thread of hope.

Reflective Time
Hymn: St Teresa's Prayer[3]

Confession of Sin
As a sign of our willingness to accept the forgiveness and mercy of our
God, you are asked to come forward to the Confessors and receive God's
forgiveness.
Singing during this

Leader: Call to Repentance
Let us together express our sorrow to God.
God of love and compassion, we see our weakness and ask your forgiveness. Help us to turn to your Son Jesus, present in this community of
faith, for the healing he alone can give. Heal the wounds and hurts that
divide us. Strengthen the fabric of our community. Amen.

Confessors extend their hands in blessing over all
The fabric of the Whole Heart is carried forward and placed in front of altar
Leader: Each and every one of us is called to live life with a big heart. We
are called to choose life and to live it to the full.

Today we have come together as a community to pray, reflect, repent
and celebrate the loving forgiveness of our God who gives us the confid-
ence to seek healing for our brokenness and the courage to continue on
our life's journey in hope. Today our parish community is stronger, since
through this celebration the threads are more firmly woven together and
we are more whole.
For your personal penance, today we ask you to choose a positive action
you will undertake in relation to one of the challenges put before us in
the scripture. Choose one that is significant for you in your life at present. Be it about:
> Trust
> Courage
> Commitment
> Empowerment
> Hope
Choose something positive you will do and do it with a big heart.

Blessing
Leader: Follow the cross towards Easter Day.
There is no other path to life
In the ordinariness of life
Let us give generously.
In the face of life's obstacles
Let us be patient and gentle.
May God give you strength and bless you, the Father, the Son and the
Holy Spirit.
All: Amen.

Leader: Let us go in peace to live life with a big heart.

Thanksgiving Song

References
1. CD *Laudate*, Music of Taizé
2. On CD *A Special Collection from Monica Brown*, Emmaus Productions 1997
3. John Michael Talbot, 1987, Birdwing Music

Reconciliation Service in Advent 1

Theme: In the desert prepare a way, the way of the Lord.

Where's the desert in our family and community?
Where's the desert in our place of work?
Where's the desert in my heart?
We gather here tonight to acknowledge the areas of our lives that are hurting and are in need of healing and forgiveness. We come to celebrate God's forgiveness of us. But firstly we need to forgive ourselves and one another. We need to focus in on the desert of our lives...
What is the desert? What words can describe one?
Hot, Barren, Lonesome, Fearsome.
The desert is where no one can live for long, where not much grows; where we become uncomfortable and want to leave.
The desert through which we must prepare the Lord's way is not the Holy Land, not in Bethlehem.
It is here ... It is now ... beginning within our own hearts.
Jesus has come. He is here with us.
And so, for Advent to be a time of welcoming, we must invite him where he has never been: into the barren, empty, lifeless spots in our lives where we've never let him before. The desert is the corner of our hearts where we are uneasy, where it hurts. It's the corner that needs Christ's forgiveness and healing and the touch of his love.
The desert puts limits on our love and prevents us from becoming more complete.
Perhaps our desert is the way we treat someone close to us:
Maybe it's a grudge we hold and refuse to let go.
Maybe it's our failure to forgive ourselves and so we carry guilty feelings through life.
Perhaps it's our failure to notice the injustices around us in family and community
Maybe it's our failure to reach out to the many victims of injustice in many parts of our world.

Tonight, we're taking time to look hard to discover the personal desert in us that is denying admittance to Christmas; to acknowledge our need for the desert to turn into an oasis so that life in all its fullness can be ours this Christmas and always.

Song: Prepare Ye The Way of the Lord[1] *or some other appropriate song of Advent*

Scripture Reading: Matthew 3:1-6 'Repent ... Prepare the way of the Lord.'

Guided Reflection/ Examination of Conscience
A Holly Leaf as the Symbol
In the tranquillity of the guided meditation tonight, we have the opportunity to meet with Jesus and to allow to surface what we need to bring to him for healing and forgiveness. Hold the leaf in your hand. I invite you to make yourself comfortable ... to enter into the peace and quiet of this sacred space ... to try to let go of the busyness of the day ... and enter into the now, the present moment. If you wish, close your eyes and focus for a moment on yourself, how you're feeling; maybe then you are ready to tune into your breathing and be still ...
Hear God speak to you: 'Be still and know I am your God.' ... Be aware of the leaf you hold in your hands ... notice its colour, shape, size ... feel its sharpness and its smoothness ... I invite you to see in this leaf a symbol of your life ... as you come before God this evening ...
Invite Jesus into this time of quiet and ask him to journey with you as you reflect on your life ... let the smooth part of the leaf be for you a symbol of all that is good in your life ... all that brings you peace and happiness...
Tell Jesus what is life-giving for you ... maybe good relationships, friendships, the ways in which you act with honesty; your generous nature; the ways you show love to those around you ... the gift of your health ... your great sense of gratitude ... your faith.
Now focus your attention on the not-so-smooth part of the leaf ... the rough edges; the stains, the flaws in it ... Let these symbolise for you now the areas of your life that are not so life-giving ... See in these sharp areas something of your life that is troubled, not at ease, in need of heal-

ing, in need of forgiveness ... maybe it's a difficult relationship ... your selfishness ... your failure to forgive someone ... your greed ... your harsh criticism and lack of compassion for someone ... your ingratitude ... Invite Jesus into these difficult, dark areas of your life ... He knows; He understands ... He wants to help you to make the rough places in your life smooth this Advent night.

Together, Jesus and you look at your family relationships ... is there anything there for which you need forgiveness? Perhaps you'd look at your relationships in your neighbourhood, in your workplace or wherever you gather with people and again see if there is anything there you wish you had done differently ... anything there you failed to do for someone? Imagine Jesus is placing his hands on your head and is saying to you, 'Receive my gift of compassion and forgiveness ... I will remove your heart of stone and give you a heart of flesh' ... Something in you reaches out for this compassion, understanding and forgiveness ... God's word echoes deep within you now: 'I will give you a new heart ... a new spirit. I exult with joy over you ...'

Be aware again of the leaf you are holding ... this leaf which now symbolises your life before God ... you in your light and darkness ... you as you are ... with your strengths and weaknesses ... all of you ... held lovingly and tenderly in God's hands.

The leaf is open ... see in this openness now a symbol of your openness to receive whatever gifts God is offering you tonight in the celebration of this sacrament ... a new heart, a new spirit ... healing of old wounds of sin and selfishness ... Hear his special words this Advent night to you ... 'Be happy at all times; give thanks for all things.'

Take the holly leaf with you as you go to one of the confessors to make your individual confession. As you return to your place, leave it at the crib, then take some grains of incense, symbolising your thanksgiving for the gift of reconciliation and wholeness, and place them in the lighted container ... so that your prayer rises like incense before God.

Reference
1. *Godspel*

Reconciliation Service in Advent 2

Welcome and Introduction
Good evening and welcome to this parish celebration of reconciliation.
What a rich opportunity we are given tonight to experience the healing
mercy of God in this sacrament. We're all well aware that Christmas is
such a busy time. There is scarcely time to go to church. There is scarcely
time to be by oneself, let alone to pray. As the body of Christ here in this
parish community, we will be entering into a time of prayer ... of reflection ... of repentance and celebration.

Our sin affects not only ourselves, but the community of the family
and parish here. When we sin, this community is less whole, has more
brokenness ... so tonight we acknowledge our brokenness as a community and we come to receive healing and forgiveness.
I invite you to stand and sing:

Song: Where healing can begin[1]

Scripture Reading: Thess 5:16-24 or John 8:1-11 or Matthew 2:1-12

Meditation / Examination of Conscience
A Star Shape is the Symbol
In the quiet of the evening we take a few moments to think about our
lives – our relationship with God, with ourselves, with each other.

We too, in the busyness of life, need to stop and to ask ourselves like
the Wise Men did: 'Where is the King' Where is Jesus for me? Where is
Jesus in all the rush and fuss as we prepare for Christmas?

As you hold the star you received on the way in, see in it a symbol of
your hopes and dreams for yourself this Advent time, as you continue on
your journey of faith. The wise men set out together ... we too go
through life in the company of others. The wise men saw the star; they
followed it. They saw it as a calling from God ... it was their guide to
where Jesus was to be found. Who or what has helped you in recent

times to find Jesus? Have you been a star in other peoples' lives pointing them to where Jesus is to be found?

What keeps you going? What gives meaning to your life? Is it keeping your eye on the star? On life's journey you get sidetracked at times.

Maybe you were drawn down ways that have not helped you to be happy. Maybe it's your failing to be reconciled with someone who has hurt you or whom you have hurt.

Perhaps you have found yourself being greedy and selfish, not caring much about the needs of others.

Maybe it's the abuse of alcohol or some other substance that leaves the family short of necessities

Perhaps, it's you being dishonest in your dealings with people.

Sometimes a cloud covers our star in life and we lose our way.

What's the cloud for you now?

Perhaps, it's your failure to forgive yourself and the carrying of guilty feelings which drags you down.

Perhaps it's a grudge you hold and refuse to let go of.

On their journey to Jesus, Herod tried in a devious way to get to the wise men by leading them astray because he wanted to destroy life. We meet many people on our journey: Some help us and some are blocks in our life. Who or what blocks you from following Jesus?

Do you ever try to put other people down as they try to live the gospel message?

Who do you block sometimes from finding their way to Jesus?

The wise men found Jesus and were overjoyed. We too want to find Jesus in each moment of each day, in every person we meet.

Maybe I fail to see Jesus in those around me – travellers, refugees, people who are different in some way?

Tonight, we come to Jesus who is loving and compassionate in this Sacrament of Reconciliation.

Just as the wise men brought gifts, we too bring the gift of our lives to him. We bring our sorrows, our regrets and our desire to keep on following the star which we know points to Jesus.

We come to meet Jesus who is our light in our moments of darkness, who is our strength in times of weakness, and who is our hope in our moments of despair.

The wise men went back by a different way so as to avoid Herod who had destructive intentions.

Tonight we too choose to go a different way, a way that is not destructive of life. Christ helps us to do that.

I now invite the confessors to go to the confessional points around the church. When you go to the priest bring the star with you; name one area in particular for which you want healing and forgiveness tonight. Return to your place by a different way; place your star in the centre of the large star in the sacred space.

As people go to confession Advent songs are sung or played very softly

Act of Sorrow
Response: Lord, we ask your forgiveness
For the times when we hurt others.
For the times when we have deliberately used others for personal gain.
For the times when we have put ourselves before others.
For the times when we have been too quick to find fault with people and passed judgement on them.
For the times we have made family relationships difficult.
For the times we have rejected and ignored God, except when we wanted something.

Closing Prayer
'Rejoice in the Lord always. I shall say it again: Rejoice. Your kindness should be known to all. The Lord is near – the peace of God that surpasses all understanding will guard your hearts and minds in Christ Jesus.' *Phillipians 4: 4-7*

Song: Rejoice in the Lord always

Reference
1. Carey Landry and NALR 1993, *I will not forget you,* Vol 2

Rituals for a Funeral

General Comment

Death remains the final surprise even when it is expected. Church people are presumed to have some inside information on death and are still regarded as knowing how to deal with it. We have privileged access to many who are strangers to church. It is our opportunity to ensure that people are met with understanding, respect and care. Until society provides some other way that is acceptable as a rite of passage, we still have the key to that exit. Some funerals come across as being rather casual, cold and impersonal.

This moment is the most precious we have – a real key moment. The very depths of mystery and humanity are revealed and must be respected. The official church view demands words on the resurrection and not a eulogy. This appears to reduce the fleshiness of faith and the sense of the incarnation. Each person is precious and different. If that is not noted at the time of death – then faith has never been 'enfleshed'. If people can meet God – this is a most important moment for such a meeting.

It is a very delicate and demanding moment and deserves great attention and effort. In many communities now, only four or five per cent are church-going, and so our approach must be very gentle and very thorough. It is a great challenge to our humanity, imagination and our faith. Any preparation for a funeral has to begin in the home. The visits must be gentle, sensitive and patient because it does take time to build up a relationship as so often 'they' are unknown to us and 'we' are unknown to them. Many people have no experience of a death in the family and we can bring our experience to them. It is most important to slow everything down. In Ireland we are always in too much of a rush with funerals. We can add to the rush and fuss if we appear with our business trappings and want everyone to get down to making arrangements immediately. It takes several visits to gather hearts and minds together towards decisions – if that is at all possible. It also helps if we 'can afford' to have two people (from the parish team) for these visits.

It is good to begin making 'check lists' available and suggestions on the second visit of an outline of what needs to be done, but it is more important to talk about the person who has died. Our task is to create an atmosphere where such talk can happen. This reminds us of the role of 'a wake' from the past. Stories need to be told. People need to be celebrated. Their significance needs some expression. Then we can move towards putting such thoughts into prayers. The Bidding Prayers delight people when they see them personalised and then it becomes easier to plan the rest of the Liturgy. Much of our church language is foreign to many people and we must make an attempt to break down this barrier and make some connections for this Service.

The moments which we structure are:
1. The Funeral Home.
2. The Reception at Church.
3. The Funeral Mass.
4. The Cemetery.

The Funeral Home

Prayers can be simple. It is important to avoid the impersonal language of the Ritual if possible and to connect with these particular people. Something personal is essential. It is good to ask the family to bless the person. It also helps if we name each member of the grieving family. We usually use a litany (an outline is included in the prayers at the graveside) which gathers together many aspects of the person's life. It is a prayer of gratitude and a real celebration of a life. In conclusion (if appropriate) we ask a person related to the deceased, to lead the group in a decade of the Rosary.

The Reception at Church

This is such an important psychological moment and needs to be done well. Sometimes it appears that this moment happens too quickly and casually. It is a key moment for the family and friends. In our experience, large numbers attend this part of the Service only and so we must make the very best of this opportunity. The Ritual offers very little for this occasion. Small gestures of participation are precious and seem to matter greatly to the family. Gentle music does matter both as the funeral comes in, and especially then during the time when people are coming up to sympathise with the family. We believe it is essential to give a Reflection or Homily which is personal and this doesn't have to be done by a priest. (In our experience, we find it most helpful when this is shared by other members of the parish team.)

1. Four candles are lit around the coffin by four members of the family. The Easter Candle is a sign of Christ as Light of our world. These candles are lit from the Paschal Candle as a symbol of how this person reflected the light of Christ in a special and unique way. This can be gently personalised.

2. Another member of the family places the Bible on the coffin. The Bible is the Word which God speaks to us. The story of this person is contained in the Bible. This person too was part of the Word, through whom God has spoken.

3. A member of the family places the Crucifix on the coffin. Words can be said to connect with the suffering of this person or this family and is linked with the suffering of Christ who is the source of strength, comfort and hope at this time.

4. Another family member blesses the coffin as some words are said on the blessing which this person was to the family and the blessing they were to the deceased.

5. Finally (if the family wishes to have a photo) another member places that photo on the coffin. The picture highlights the profiles/memories, we have in our own minds on this occasion.

We gather this together in the general prayers leading to Readings and a personal Reflection. We follow that with personal Bidding Prayers rather than the 'Lord have mercy' response in the Ritual. We conclude by inviting some relative or neighbour to lead us in a decade of the Rosary, or sometimes alternate with the two sides of the church. Our last gesture then is to gather this person and all the congregation into a blessing. We offer a simple and gentle Confession at the end but very few avail of the offer.

The Funeral Mass

We begin the Funeral Mass by making the link with the previous evening. This is done by inviting the family to light the candles around the coffin again. We need to remember that many people are unfamiliar and uncomfortable at Mass. Many don't know what to do. We must make everything as easy as possible. It is good to have a link person or commentator or support person to 'guide' those who have a specific task at the Liturgy. It does help to 'model' a community way of doing things on such a day. (In fact there is no way any priest can do all that is necessary in funeral preparation and the more the general community is involved the better.) It is so good to involve the wider family in taking part and to integrate all that happens (including the songs). It is so important to have someone of the local community who can escort people up to read or bring up the gifts and stand with them. It always helps to call by name the person or persons who have been assigned to a task. Bidding Prayers should be personal. The homily really has to focus on this person and this family and not just any general theme. This is where real 'incarnation' has to happen. Words on the resurrection alone are inadequate. We also need to show great respect and care for those present knowing that this is the only time many are in church.

The final prayers again should be adapted. The language in the Ritual is stilted. These final prayers over the coffin can be led by a member of the community. The family can be invited to bless and incense the coffin, which shows real respect for the person and for the family.

At the Graveside

We use the following litany at the graveside, with changes appropriate to the person and the family. It is usually good if there is a copy for everyone.

Litany for …

For …, a very special person with a gentle spirit of warm love; We thank you, Lord.

For her unassuming generosity and great presence to everyone; We thank you, Lord.

For her love and care for all; We thank you, Lord.

For her devotion to her family; We thank you, Lord.

For her great regard for this community at ...; We thank you, Lord.

For her interest in so many things but especially her love of people; We thank you, Lord.

For her strong faith which was obvious to everyone; We thank you, Lord.

For the daughter she was; We thank you, Lord.

For the sister she was to ...; We thank you, Lord.

For the wife she was to ...; We thank you, Lord.

For the mother she was to ...; We thank you, Lord.

For the grandmother she was to ...; We thank you, Lord.

For the home she made; We thank you, Lord.

For the friend and neighbour she was; We thank you, Lord.

For her commitment and participation in her local community; We thank you, Lord.

For her long service in her work place ...; We thank you, Lord.

For her presence in all the ministries in the parish; We thank you, Lord.

For the woman who quietly and happily enjoyed herself at ...; We thank you, Lord.

For the woman who died too quickly for all of us; We thank you, Lord.

For the lady of faith who inspired all of us; We thank you, Lord.

To God we say: Thank you for this person who meant so much to so many.

All Together:

May the strength of God pilot us.

May the wisdom of God instruct us.

May the hand of God protect us.

May the Word of God direct us.

May the love of God give us peace.

May that love of God be always with us today and every day.

Amen.

A Litany of Remembrance
In the rising of the sun and its going down – We remember.
In the blowing of the wind and in the chill of winter – We remember.
In the appearances of new life in spring – We remember.
In the blueness of the sky and in the warmth of summer – We remember.
In the rustling of the leaves and the beauty of autumn – We remember.
In the beginning of the year and when it ends – We remember.
When we are lost and sick at heart – We remember.
When we have joys we yearn to share – We remember.
So long as we live shall …. live,
for she is part of our lives.

It is very important to be there for the family in the weeks and months after-wards. The connections that are made with the family at this time are enduring.

The Celebration of the Sacrament of Confirmation

General Comment

Confirmation is a key moment for the faith community but the reality is something different. The celebration doesn't relate to the people present and their experience. Generally, the adults are bored and disconnected from what is going on. There is a lack of reverence and an absence of a sense of the sacred. We found that there was an urgent need to do something with the Ritual to make this moment more significant in a way that would help participants to be in touch with God, church and community.

The parish team and Parish Pastoral Council decided to do something about this issue. A lack of reverence was felt to be partly due to the length of the ceremony and the lack of involvement by the adults. We believed that a standard should be set which would aim at creating a sense of the sacred and some realisation of the importance of the moment. We decided to concentrate on the Sacrament and allow it to stand on its own (without Mass). We decided to emphasise elements of the Sacrament by emphasising Enrolment, Service of Light and the role of parish community, parents, school and children. The format (below) is what has evolved over the years and which we have found to be good.

We have evaluated the ceremony each year with parents, teachers and the parish pastoral council. They have agreed that the ceremony is more focused; more participatory; holds the attention of all; is more reverent; the language is more understandable and appropriate; is shorter and more to the point. This format has been in use for five years and has been recommended by the area bishop to many other parishes.

Opening Hymn and Procession

Words of Welcome: (Member of Parish team)

Bishop's Welcome: The Bishop greets all, says a few introductory words and then leads all in prayer:

Let us pray:
Lord fulfil your promise,
Send your Holy Spirit to make us witnesses
Before the world to the Good News
Proclaimed by Jesus Christ,
Who lives and reigns with you and the Holy Spirit,
One God for ever and ever.
All: Amen.

Hymn: Here I am Lord[1]

Resume of the Journey so Far
A member of the parish team gives a short summary of the preparation process throughout the year.

The Enquiry
A member of the Parish community asks the following questions of the young people on their understanding and commitment.
Are you serious about being confirmed?
Response: I am

Do you understand that this means you must give a place to God in your lives?
Response: I do.

Do you realise that Confirmation only makes sense if you make some link with the parish community during the year?
Response: I do.

Have you any intention of trying to find out what is expected of you as a young Christian Adult?
Response: I have.

Do you accept that you should be responsible for giving good example to the other children?
Response: I do.

Do you accept that you must grow up now and see how best you can contribute to the wider community where you live?
Response: I do.

Do you see the link between being confirmed and bringing the love of Christ to others?
Response: I do.

Bishop: We give thanks to God for your commitment and we pray that the Holy Spirit will guide you to live it to the full.

Sponsors: As representatives of the community of faith we promise to be an example to these young people in our faith and practice.

Teachers: We the teachers, have been privileged to help these young people to a deeper understanding of God's kingdom. Our wish and our prayer for them is that they will commit themselves to the spread of God's Kingdom. May the light that we have lit for them in our classrooms grow into a great flame of goodness in their hearts. Amen.

Candidates: We thank the teachers and ask God to bless them. They have given us wisdom and understanding and learning. May they be rewarded in heaven and on earth for keeping the light of faith burning in our lives. Amen.

Parents: These are our sons and daughters given to us by God, to be loved and cherished, healed and helped, scolded and forgiven, advised and warned, to be led by us into the fullness of manhood and womanhood. Amen.

Candidates: Dear Parents, sponsors and teachers, we thank you for all you have done for us in our lives. We thank you for the love you have shown us and the sacrifices you have made for us. We thank you for helping us to prepare for Confirmation. We thank you especially for sharing your faith with us. We will now publicly proclaim your faith as our faith.

Renewal of Baptismal Promises
A parishioner invites all to make a profession of their faith.

1. Do you believe in God the Father almighty?
Response: I do. I acknowledge him to be the Source of all life. I believe that he has called us by name.

2. Do you believe in God the Son?
Response: I do. I believe that Jesus Christ, the Risen Lord is alive and with us always to the end of time.

3. Do you believe in God the Holy Spirit?
Response: I do. I believe that he is with the Church, and with each of us, giving us direction and strength.

4. Do you recognise and reject the evil in our world and refuse to be led astray by it?
Response: I promise to live well.
I promise to give time to prayer.
I promise to be true to Jesus Christ at home, in school and in play.
I promise to witness to my faith by the way I live.
I promise to reject violence and vandalism in all its forms.
I promise to work in our neighbourhood to make the environment better for everyone.
I promise to care for those who are sad, lonely and weary.
I promise to bring happiness and laughter, rather than sadness and misery to people near us.

This then is our faith. We are proud to profess it.

The Word of God: scripture reading recommended by Presiding Bishop

Homily

The Naming and Confirming

Naming
Each candidate calls out his/her name and comes out in a long line down the aisles. A parent and sponsor stands behind them.
Candidates with parent/sponsor approach the Bishop for confirmation.

Bishop: My dear friends, in Baptism God our Father gave the new birth of eternal life to his chosen sons and daughters. Let us pray to our Father that he will pour out the Holy Spirit to strengthen his sons and daughters with his gifts and anoint them to be more like Christ, the Son of God ... *(Silent prayer for a moment)* All powerful God, Father of our Lord Jesus Christ, by water and the Holy Spirit, you freed your sons and daughters from sin and gave them new life. Send your Holy Spirit upon them to be their helper and guide. Give them the Spirit of wisdom and understanding, the spirit of right judgement and courage, the spirit of knowledge and reverence. Fill them with the spirit of wonder and awe in your presence. We ask this through Christ our Lord, Amen.

Anointing with Chrism
Bishop: Be sealed with the gift of the Holy Spirit.
Candidate: Amen.
Bishop: Peace be with you.
Candidate: And also with you.

Participatory singing quietly takes place during the confirming.
A member of the Parish team reflects on the significance of the anointing.

Intercessory Prayers
Led by representatives of candidates, parents, teachers and parish community.

Named, Called, Confirmed and now Sent
Some concluding remarks by a member of the parish team.

Concluding Prayer

Lord, help those you have anointed by your Spirit. Support them through every stage of their lives' journey. And by their works of kindness, build up the community in holiness and joy. Grant this through Christ our Lord. Amen.

Solemn Blessing
Bishop:

God our Father, complete the work you have begun in these young people and keep the gifts of the Holy Spirit alive in their hearts. Make them ready to live out what they promised and make them eager to do your will. May they never be ashamed to proclaim to the world the mystery of God's presence among us all. Amen.

May the blessing of Almighty God, the Father, the Son and the Holy Spirit, come down upon you and remain with you forever.
Amen.

Go in peace to love and serve the Lord.
Thanks be to God.

Concluding hymn and procession

References
1. Dan Schutte SJ and NALR, 1981

A House Blessing

General Comment
When a family moves into a new home in the parish, an ideal opportunity presents itself for parish outreach. One or two people from the visitation team call to the home to welcome the family on behalf of the parish. In doing so, we are recognising this as a key moment not to be missed. At such visits, people are offered the opportunity to have their home blessed. A candle, St Brigid's cross, a bottle of holy water and copies of the blessing text are brought along to be used and then left to each family. If there are children in the home it is important to involve them in the ritual of blessing. This blessing is always much appreciated by those who experience it. It is good to personalise the blessing and involve the names of people that matter to the family.

Opening Prayer
Lord, our God, come and bless this house which is now to be the home of the family. Surround this family home with your Holy Spirit. May all its four sides be protected with your power so that peace may be present here. May God's blessing protect this home and all who live here.

As each section is blessed someone goes to that place in the home and sprinkles it with holy water.

Bless the doorway. May all who come to it be treated with respect and kindness.
Bless the rooms of this house. May each of them be holy and filled with the spirit of happiness.
Bless the living room. May this family live within it as people of peace.
Bless the kitchen where the family cook and eat. May all their meals be occasions of friendship and fun.
Bless the bathroom. May the spirit of health and healing live there and teach each one to honour, respect and love their bodies.

Bless each of the bedrooms. May the family find rest and refreshment in these rooms.

Let us now pause and pray in silence as we call down the blessing of God on this house which is now the home of the family ...

May the door of this home always be open to those in need.
May the light of God's presence shine brightly in this home and be a blessing to all who will live here and for everyone who will come to this home.
We pray together:
On this house your blessing Lord.
On this house your grace bestow.
On this house your blessing Lord.
May it come and never go.
Bringing peace and joy and happiness,
Bringing love that knows no end.
On this house your blessing Lord
May it come and never go.

Hold up St Brigid's Cross
May Brigid bless this house wherein you dwell.
Bless every fireside, every wall and floor,
Bless every heart that beats beneath its roof,
And every tongue and mind forever more.

And May God's blessing rest upon each one of you, in the name of the Father, and of the Son, and of the Holy Spirit. Amen.

Notes

Notes

Notes

Notes

Notes

Notes